FRANÇOISE AND PAULINE BAYLE
With the collaboration of Gaspard Walter

NEW YORK
IN 50 MAPS

750
PLACES
FOR URBAN
ADVENTURES

UNIVERSE

DISCOVER THE 750 BEST ADDRESSES OF THE CITY IN THIS UNIQUE AND ESSENTIAL GUIDE:

The unmissable, the most secret, and the authors' discoveries and personal favorites. Even before you set foot in the city, this guide will take you on a journey, thanks to the clever and colorful maps.

Featuring talented illustrators from around the world such as Jon Burgerman, Mari Araki, Niark1, and Lorenzo Petrantoni.

A SIMPLE SYSTEM OF PICTOGRAMS TO HELP GUIDE THE READER

♥ Authors' personal favorite

$ Inexpensive
$$ Average
$$$ Expensive
$$$$ Very expensive
$$$$$ Luxury

01 NEW YORK WITHOUT THE TOURISTS

Hypnotized by the skyscrapers, the only New York that most tourists will see is the heart of Manhattan: Central Park, and 5th Avenue. Yet behind the buildings or on the other side of the East River, there hides a more authentic, more private New York. Cobblestone streets and brick walls, artists' lofts and hipster bars, mysterious beaches and minuscule museums: the city has many other faces to show curious visitors.

❶ DUMBO ♥
With its brick buildings and cobblestone streets, this very photogenic neighborhood, crossed by the Manhattan Bridge, served as the backdrop for Sergio Leone's masterpiece *Once Upon a Time in America*.
North of York St. station, Brooklyn, NY 11201. Subway: F to York St.

❷ GREENPOINT
A neighborhood that's growing hipper by the minute; dotted with bars, vintage stores, and Polish shops.
Around the Nassau Av. station and the length of Manhattan Av., Brooklyn, NY 11222. Subway: G to Nassau Av. or Greenpoint Av.

❸ BUSHWICK
Graffiti, bars, pizzerias, and artists' lofts in this hyperhip neighborhood.
In the rectangle formed by Flushing Ave., Cypress Ave., Cooper St., and Broadway, Brooklyn, NY 11237. Subway: L to Morgan Av.

❹ WILLIAMSBURG ♥
Bearded, tattooed guys wearing glasses and checked flannel shirts: the world's hipster capital.
Between the East River, McCarren Park, Bushwick Ave. and Flushing Ave., Brooklyn, NY 11211.
Subway: L to Lorimer St.

❺ BROOKLYN WATERFRONT
An unimpeded view over Midtown and the Manhattan skyline.
Between N 11th St. and N 12th St., the length of the East River, Brooklyn, NY 11211. Subway: L to Bedford Av.

❻ BROOKLYN HEIGHTS PROMENADE
For a spectacular view of the Manhattan skyline, the Financial District, the East River, and the Brooklyn Bridge.
From Remsen St. to Middagh St., the length of the East River, Brooklyn, NY 11201. Subway: N, R to Clark St.

❼ VINEGAR HILL
Quiet cobblestone streets and colorful facades.
In the square formed by the East River, West St., Front St., and Bridge St., Brooklyn, NY 11201.
Subway: F to York St.

❽ BRIGHTON BEACH/LITTLE ODESSA
Russia in New York, on the seashore.
Between Brighton Beach Ave. and the beach, Brooklyn, NY 11235.
Subway: B, Q to Brighton Beach

❾ DEAD HORSE BAY ♥
This beach is covered with centuries-old rubbish! Antique perfume bottles, ceramic pieces—one of the strangest and most bewitching places in New York.
Gateway National Recreation Area, Brooklyn, NY 11234.
Subway: Q to Neck Road, then B2 or Q35 Bus to Flatbush Ave

❿ EAST VILLAGE
Punk stores, tattoo shops, and a laid back attitude.
In the rectangle formed by 4th Ave., E 14th St., the East River, and E Houston St., New York, NY 10003.
Subway: 4, 6 to Astor Pl.

⓫ ROOSEVELT ISLAND
A walk through one of the city's least-known neighborhoods.
Roosevelt Island, New York, NY 10044. Subway: F to Roosevelt Island

⓬ GOVERNORS ISLAND
Expansive lawns and an open view over the bay and the Financial District.
Governors Island, New York, NY 11231. By ferry from 10 South St.

⓭ FLUSHING, OR MANDARIN TOWN
One of the largest Chinese communities outside of China.
Around Flushing–Main St. station, Flushing, NY 11354.
Subway: 7 to Flushing–Main St.

⓮ CITY ISLAND
White sails, wooden houses, New England atmosphere, and excellent seafood.
Bronx, NY 10464.
Subway: Northbound 6 to Pelham Bay Park, then Bx29 Bus to City Island Ave./Fordham St.

⓯ STATEN ISLAND
Free round trip from the bustle of the Financial District to the calm of Staten Island.
NY 10301. By boat from the South Ferry Terminal.

02 15 SITES TO SEE BEFORE YOU DIE

New York is an immense city; a city so rich that it can be a challenge to even know where to start. Since no visit to the Big Apple would be complete without gazing toward the tip of the Empire State Building, without a stroll on the Brooklyn Bridge or a glance over Manhattan from the crown of the Statue of Liberty, here is the list of places that must absolutely be seen, before going on to discover the rest with no regrets.

❶ EMPIRE STATE BUILDING ♥
A symbol of the city and an art deco masterpiece; its antenna reaches a height of 1,454 feet.
350 5th Ave., New York, NY 10118.
Subway: N, Q, R to 34 St.–Herald Sq.

❷ STATUE OF LIBERTY NATIONAL MONUMENT ♥
Flame pointed toward the sky, a symbol of the city, of America, and of freedom. On the list of UNESCO World Heritage sites since 1984.
Liberty Island: Boarding from Battery Park, 75 Battery Pl., New York, NY 10280.
Subway: 1 to South Ferry

❸ FLATIRON BUILDING ♥
A skyscraper emblematic of New York, with a unique profile that looks like an iron.
175 5th Ave., New York, NY 10010.
Subway: N, R to 23 St.

❹ CHRYSLER BUILDING
One of New Yorkers' favorite skyscrapers, with its famous spire and metal structure.
405 Lexington Ave., New York, NY 10174. Subway: 4, 5, 6 to Grand Central–42 St.

❺ GRAND CENTRAL TERMINAL
The constellations of the zodiac stand out on the turquoise ceiling of the main hall in this iconic building inaugurated in 1871.
87 E 42nd St., New York, NY 10017.
Subway: 4, 5, 6 to Grand Central–42 St.

❻ TRINITY CHURCH
Gothic Revival-style church, inaugurated in 1846.
75 Broadway, New York, NY 10006.
Subway: 4, 5 to Wall St.

❼ BROOKLYN BRIDGE ♥
One of the most beautiful and oldest bridges in New York.
New York, NY–Brooklyn, NY
Subway: 4, 5, 6 to Brooklyn Bridge–City Hall

❽ RADIO CITY MUSIC HALL
Art Deco building inaugurated in 1932; the main auditorium can seat over 6,000 spectators.
1260 Ave. of the Americas, New York, NY 10020.
Subway: B, D, F, M to 47–50 Sts–Rockefeller Center

❾ YANKEE STADIUM
Home stadium of the NY Yankees, one of the two famous New York baseball teams.
1 E 161st St., Bronx, NY 10451.
Subway: B, D, 4 to 161 St.–Yankee Stadium

❿ *CHARGING BULL*
Bronze sculpture by the artist Arturo Di Modica, a Wall St. icon.
Bowling Green Park, Broadway and Morris St., New York, NY 10004.
Subway: 4, 5, 6 to Bowling Green

⓫ 9/11 MEMORIAL & MUSEUM
A work dealing with the themes of silence and absence, dedicated to the 2,977 victims of the attacks that took place on September 11, 2001.
180 Greenwich St., New York, NY 10007. Subway: 1 to Cortlandt St.

⓬ NEW YORK PUBLIC LIBRARY
Over 53 million books and documents are found in this library!
5th Ave. at 42nd St., New York, NY 10018. Subway: 7 to 5 Av.

⓭ ROCKEFELLER CENTER
There are 19 buildings on this 22 acre complex, the highest reaching 850 ft.
Rockefeller Plaza, New York, NY 10111.
Subway: B, D, F, M to 47–50 Sts–Rockefeller Center

⓮ THE UNISPHERE
The unofficial symbol of Queens, the height of this sculpture representing Earth is equivalent to a 12-story building.
Flushing Meadows-Corona Park, Flushing, NY 11355.
Subway: 7 to Mets-Willets Point Station

⓯ *WILLIAMSBURG BRIDGE*
Metal bridge over the East River; very popular with cyclists and joggers.
Brooklyn, NY 11211.
Subway: J, M, Z to Marcy Av.

03 A DAY AT THE MUSEUM

New York is one of the planet's major cultural capitals, with over 130 museums and 1,500 art galleries. From medieval art to modern art, masterpieces of ancient Egypt or historical artifacts: hours of inspiration await you in the Big Apple's museums!

❶ ELLIS ISLAND IMMIGRATION MUSEUM
A moving memorial to what was long ago the processing center for immigrants arriving from Europe.
Ellis Island, Jersey City, NY 07305.
Access by boat from Manhattan

❷ NATIONAL MUSEUM OF THE AMERICAN INDIAN
Some million objects coming from Amerindian sites collected by G. G. Heye.
1 Bowling Green, New York, NY 10004.
Subway: 4, 5 to Bowling Green

❸ THE NEW MUSEUM ♥
Contemporary art in a building designed by Japanese architects Kazuyo Sejima and Ryue Nishizawa.
235 Bowery, New York, NY 10002.
Subway: F to 2nd Av.

❹ AMERICAN FOLK ART MUSEUM
A museum that gathers together 5,000 pieces of folk art.
2 Lincoln Sq., New York, NY 10023.
Subway: 1 to 66 St.–Lincoln Center

❺ THE MUSEUM OF MODERN ART (MOMA) ♥
An impressive collection ranging from the nineteenth century to today.
11 W 53rd St., New York, NY 10019.
Subway: E, M to 5 Av.–53 St.

❻ TENEMENT MUSEUM
Dedicated to the history of European immigrants in New York.
103 Orchard St., New York, NY 10002.
Subway: F to Delancey St.

❼ INTERNATIONAL CENTER OF PHOTOGRAPHY
An amazing museum, school, and research center devoted to photography.
250 Bowery, New York, NY 10012.
Subway: F to 2 Av.

❽ THE FRICK COLLECTION
This mansion is home to one of the world's finest private collections, including masterpieces of European art.
1 E 70th St., New York, NY 10021.
Subway: 6 to 68 St.–Hunter College

❾ THE METROPOLITAN MUSEUM OF ART ♥
Encyclopedic collections in one of the world's largest museums.
1000 5th Ave., New York, NY 10028.
Subway: 4, 5, 6 to 86 St.

❿ THE CLOISTERS
A tribute to the art and architecture of the Middle Ages.
99 Margaret Corbin Dr., New York, NY 10040. Subway: A to Dyckman St.

⓫ GUGGENHEIM MUSEUM
A modern art museum in an architectural gem designed by Frank Lloyd Wright.
1071 5th Ave., New York, NY 10128.
Subway: 4, 5, 6 to 86 St.

⓬ NEUE GALERIE NEW YORK
A sublime collection of German and Austrian art, housed in the former Vanderbilt mansion.
1048 5th Ave., New York, NY 10028.
Subway: 4, 5, 6 to 86 St.

⓭ LOUIS ARMSTRONG HOUSE MUSEUM
Souvenirs, photos, and recordings in the house of the famous trumpet player.
34-56 107th St., Corona, NY 11368.
Subway: 7 to 103 St.–Corona Plaza

⓮ WHITNEY MUSEUM OF AMERICAN ART
Twentieth- and twenty-first-century American art.
99 Gansevoort St., New York, NY 10014.
Subway: L to 8 Av.

⓯ BROOKLYN MUSEUM
A magnificent fine arts museum, the second largest museum in New York and, although not well-known, one of the country's most prestigious art institutions.
200 Eastern Pkwy, Brooklyn, NY 11238. Subway: 2, 3 to Eastern Pkwy–Brooklyn Museum

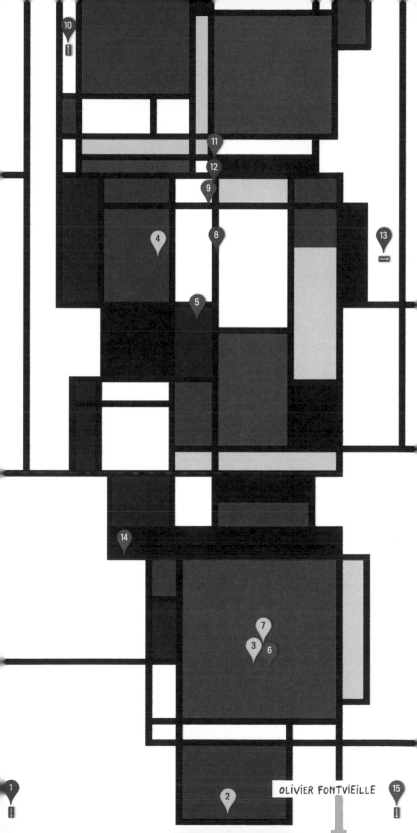

OLIVIER FONTVIEILLE

04 ART ATTACK

Over the years New York has emerged as one of the main centers of artistic creation. Today the hundreds of galleries that inhabit Chelsea, the Lower East Side, and Brooklyn perfectly reflect the diversity and richness of contemporary art.

❶ JEN BEKMAN GALLERY
A gallery that democratizes contemporary art. Exhibits include works by Christine Collins, Joseph Holmes, Sarah McKenzie, Laura Plageman, Mike Sinclair, Jessica Snow, and Kurt Tong.
6 Spring St., New York, NY 10012.
Subway: 6 to Spring St.

❷ GAGOSIAN GALLERY
Heavyweights of contemporary art, such as Richard Serra and Yayoi Kusama, exhibit here.
555 W 24th St., New York, NY 10011.
Subway: C, E to 23 St.

❸ METRO PICTURES
A gallery with bold installations, which shows the works of Cindy Sherman and Robert Longo, among others.
519 W 24th St., New York, NY 10011.
Subway: C, E to 23 St.

❹ MATTHEW MARKS GALLERY
A discerning selection of contemporay works, including those of Nan Goldin, Ellsworth Kelly, and Brice Marden.
523 W 24th St., New York, NY 10001.
Subway: C, E to 23 St.

❺ DIA:CHELSEA
Gallery hosting temporary installations, artists' talks, and readings.
535 W 22nd St., New York, NY 10011.
Subway: C, E to 23 St.

❻ AGORA GALLERY
A prestigious space showing a wide range of contemporary artists.
530 W 25th St., New York, NY 10001.
Subway: C, E to 23 St.

❼ DAVID ZWIRNER GALLERY
All Manhattanites rush to his exhibitions.
525 W 19th St., New York, NY 10011.
Subway: A, C, E, L to 14 St.

❽ LUHRING AUGUSTINE GALLERY
Founded in 1985, the gallery exhibits a quality selection of contemporary works from major names.
531 W 24th St., New York, NY 10011.
Subway: C, E to 23 St.

❾ SEAN KELLY GALLERY
A gallerist who made his name by presenting unconventional installations.
475 10th Ave., New York, NY 10018.
Subway: C, E to 34 St.

❿ JACK SHAINMAN GALLERY
Stroll through this spacious, light-filled space to admire works by Kerry James Marshall, Odili Donald Odita, and Nick Cave.
513 W 20th St., New York, NY 10011.
Subway: C, E to 23 St.

⓫ LEHMANN MAUPIN GALLERY
An international and eclectic mix of acclaimed contemporary artists.
536 W 22nd St., New York, NY 10001.
Subway: C, E to 23 St.

⓬ CONTEMPORARY AFRICAN ART GALLERY
Discover today's African art. Some thirty artists, showcasing diverse techniques: wood or stone sculptures, oil paintings, ink or pastel drawings, etchings, installations. Works by Alexander "Skunder" Boghossian, El Anatsui, Mor Faye, Iba Ndiaye, Henry Munyaradzi and John Takawira.
330 W. 108th at Riverside Dr., New York, NY 10025.
Subway: 1 to Cathedral Pkwy.

⓭ SCARAMOUCHE
A young gallery that focuses on performances and conceptual art.
52 Orchard St., New York, NY 10002.
Subway: D to Grand St.

⓮ CHEIM & READ
Over 5000 sq. ft. of exhibition space in Chelsea. Look for works by Diane Arbus, Louise Bourgeois, Jenny Holzer, Milton Resnick, and Pat Steir.
547 W 25th St., New York, NY 10001.
Subway: C, E to 23 St.

⓯ ON STELLAR RAYS
Shows the works of up-and-coming-artists. The name of this gallery reflects a certain vision of art as a form of cultural physics. It comes from the book *On the Stellar Rays*, in which Al-Kindi, a ninth-century Muslim scholar and philosopher, revealed the first Greek theories of physics and optics.
1 Rivington St., New York, NY 10002.
Subway: J to Bowery

PHILIPPE HALABURDA

05 SUBWAY SITES

It's impossible to discover New York without taking the subway tunnels. Logistical puzzles, walls peeling from the dampness and suffocating heat. While the New York subway might not be attractive, it never stops, running 24 hours a day, and remains the best way to get from one neighborhood to another.

1 RECORD MART $$
A vintage record store, hidden within the subway tunnels.
7 Times Sq. IRT subway mezzanine, New York, NY 10036.
Subway: N, Q, R, S, 1, 2, 3, 7 to Times Sq.–42nd St.

2 NEW YORK TRANSIT MUSEUM $
Located in a 1930s station, it's devoted to the New York subway.
Boerum Pl. and Schermerhorn St., Brooklyn, NY 11201.
Subway: 2, 3, 4 to Borough Hall

3 *THE SEVEN YEAR ITCH* SUBWAY GRATE
A replica of this subway grate was used in the studio for the famous scene in Billy Wilder's film *The Seven Year Itch*, in which a breeze lifts up Marilyn Monroe's white dress.
Lexington Ave. and E 52nd St., New York, NY 10022.
Subway: 6 to 51 St.

4 ASTOR PL. STATION
A few remains of the original decor: small ceramic plaques picturing a beaver, symbol of the Astor family's fortune.
E 8th St. and Lafayette St., New York, NY 10003. Subway: 6 to Astor Pl.

5 58 JORALEMON ST.
A subway vent disguised as a Greek Revival-style brick home. The door serves as an emergency exit.
58 Joralemon St., Brooklyn, NY 11201.
Subway: 4, 5 to Borough Hall

6 CITY HALL HIDDEN STATION ♥
A forgotten subway station, an architectural marvel from 1904.
To catch a glimpse: At the terminus (Brooklyn Bridge–City Hall, 6 train), stay on the train; it will cross the former station before turning around to continue in the other direction.

7 GRAND CENTRAL MARKET $$$
A market inside the station, in a small gallery joining Lexington to the main hall.
Grand Central Terminal, 89 E 42nd St., New York, NY 10017.
Subway: S, 4, 5, 6, 7 to Grand Central–42nd St.

8 WHISPERING GALLERY, GRAND CENTRAL TERMINAL
A very peculiar ceramic vaulted ceiling: whisper into a corner facing the wall and a person in a diagonally opposite position will hear you perfectly.
89 E 42nd St., New York, NY 10017.
Subway: S, 4, 5, 6, 7 to Grand Central–42nd St.

9 SMITH - 9TH STS STATION
With a platform perched at nearly 88 ft., Smith-9th Sts is the highest elevated station in the world.
9th St., Brooklyn, NY 11215.
Subway: to Smith-9 Sts

10 GRAND CENTRAL TERMINAL ♥
The station's ceiling has been restored, but if you look carefully (follow the line that crosses the constellation of Cancer) you can identify a small black rectangle that has been preserved. This black has been analyzed, revealing a 90% cigarette tar content.
87 E 42nd St., New York, NY 10017.
Subway: S, 4, 5, 6, 7 to Grand Central–42nd St.

11 WORTH ST. STATION
The Worth St. station, on the 6 train, has been closed to the public since 1962. By looking through the train window between Canal St. and Brooklyn Bridge–City Hall, you can glimpse it in the shadows.

12 E 180TH ST. STATION
One of the most beautiful New York stations, built in the style of an Italian villa.
E 180th St. and Morris Park Ave., Bronx, NY 10460. Subway: 2, 5 to E 180 St.

13 231ST ST. STATION
Admire the work by Felipe Galindo, *Magic Realism in Kingsbridge* (2008).
W 231st St. and Broadway, Bronx, NY 10463. Subway: 1 to 231 St.

14 135TH ST.
View the glass mosaic by Willie Birch, *Harlem Timeline* (1995).
W 135th St. and Malcolm X Blvd, New York, NY 10037.
Subway: 2, 3 to 135th St.

15 FLUSHING - MAIN ST. STATION
Admire the ceramic-tile mural installed by Ik-Joong Kang, *Happy World* (1999).
Main St. and Roosevelt Ave., Flushing, NY 11354. Subway: 7 to Flushing–Main St.

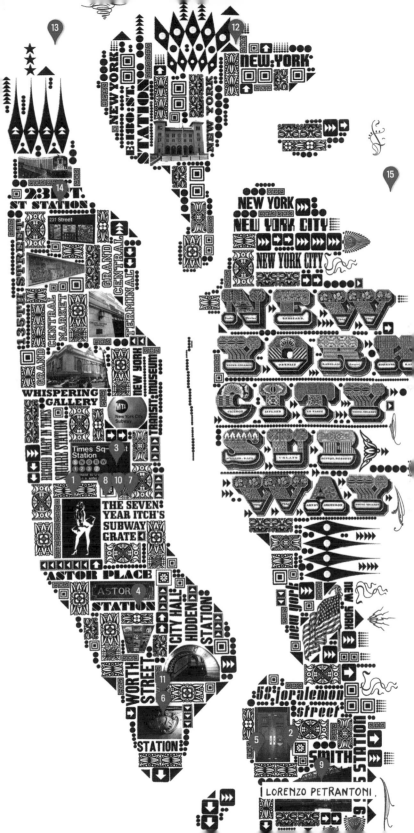

06 NEW YORK, VERTICAL CITY

A symbol of the United States and American gigantism, for two centuries New York has been the laboratory and favorite playground of architects from around the world. Brick walls sit next to smoked-glass facades; sidewalks are lined with alternating Victorian houses, vertiginous buildings, and rehabilitated industrial spaces. The city offers the greatest architectural diversity of the planet.

① MORRIS-JUMEL MANSION
A magnificent Georgian-style house, built in 1765, which served as George Washington's headquarters for five weeks in 1776.
65 Jumel Terrace, New York, NY 10032.
Subway: C to 163 St.–Amsterdam Av.

② ROCKEFELLER CENTER
An immense architectural complex consisting of some nineteen buildings.
45 Rockefeller Plaza, New York, NY 10111.
Subway: 47-50 Sts.–Rockefeller Center

③ CASTLE CLINTON NATIONAL MONUMENT
The only fort in Manhattan that has been saved. Its cannons were never used!
Battery Park, New York, NY 10004.
Subway: R to Whitehall St.

④ CUNARD BUILDING ♥
Designed by Benjamin Morris in a Neo-Renaissance style, it houses one of the most splendid halls of the city.
25 Broadway, New York, NY 10004.
Subway: 5 to Bowling Green

⑤ EQUITABLE BUILDING
Its 40 stories provoked a new building code in 1916, imposing recesses on the top floors of skyscrapers so that the streets below would not be too dark.
120 Broadway, New York, NY 10271.
Subway: 4, 5 to Wall St.

⑥ KING OF GREENE ST. ♥
One of the most extraordinary examples of a building with cast-iron facade, imagined by I. F. Duckworth.
72 Greene St., New York, NY 10012.
Subway: N, R to Prince St.

⑦ PATCHIN PLACE
A Greenwich Village impasse lined with a row of ten brick houses in which a number of famous writers once lived, including Randolph Bourne, John Silas Reed, and Djuna Barnes.
Access via 10th St. (between Greenwich Ave. and 6th Ave.), New York, NY 10011.
Subway: F to 14th St.

⑧ GRAND CENTRAL TERMINAL
Its main concourse, immortalized by Cary Grant in *North by Northwest*, is a beauty!
89 E 42nd St., New York, NY 10017.
Subway: S, 4, 5, 6, 7 to Grand Central–42nd St.

⑨ HEARST TOWER
A 597 ft. glass tower, built on the base of an unfinished 1928 building.
300 W 57th St., New York, NY 10019.
Subway: A, B, C, D, 1 to 59 St.–Columbus Circle

⑩ BAYARD-CONDICT BUILDING
The only New York construction by Louis Sullivan, master of the Chicago school and one of the first architects to build a New York skyscraper.
65 Bleecker St., New York, NY 10023.
Subway: B, D, F, M, 6 to Broadway-Lafayette St.

⑪ MERCHANT'S HOUSE MUSEUM
An 1832 house kept intact inside and out.
29 E 4th St., New York, NY 10003.
Subway: 6 to Astor Pl.

⑫ ONE WORLD TRADE CENTER
A glass tower of 1791 ft., the highest skyscraper in the Northern Hemisphere.
1 World Trade Center, New York, NY 10007. Subway: E to World Trade Center

⑬ WOOLWORTH BUILDING ♥
Inaugurated in 1913, it's one of the oldest and most graceful skyscrapers in New York.
233 Broadway, New York, NY 10007.
Subway: E to World Trade Center

⑭ CUSHMAN ROW
One of the most handsome rows of facades from the 1840s: Greek Revival-style houses built by a wealthy merchant, Alonzo Cushman; windows crowned by cast-iron laurel wreaths and pineapples on iron newels.
406 to 418 W 20th St., New York, NY 10011.
Subway: C, E to 23 St.

⑮ NEW YORK STOCK EXCHANGE
The heart of the world's economy, in a 1903 neoclassical building.
11 Wall St., New York, NY 10005.
Subway: 2, 3, 4, 5 to Wall St.

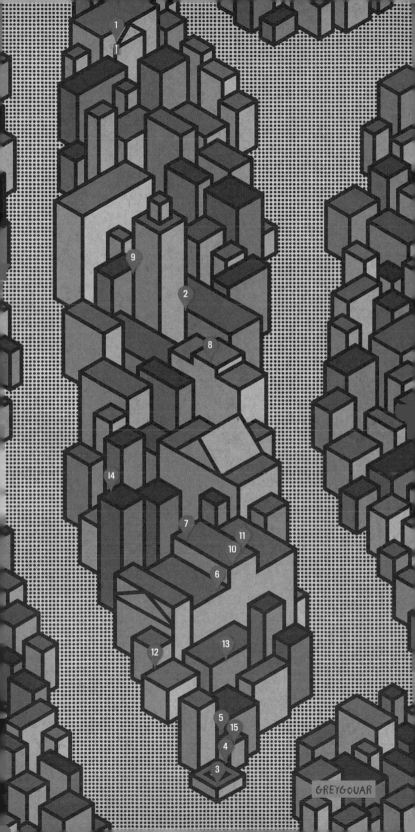

07 PAGE TURNERS

Like to read? Treat yourself to a walk through stacks of books and settle comfortably into the recesses of a leather chair in the relaxing atmosphere of these silent spaces. Rich with a unique cultural and literary heritage, New York's history has been described by writers in the nineteenth century (Walt Whitman, Herman Melville, and Washington Irving, for example), and in the twentieth century it was the stage of profound upheaval, reflected in the literature of F. Scott Fitzgerald and Paul Auster. Explore the streets of this exceptional city in search of the constantly renewed stories that it inspires.

❶ ST. MARK'S BOOKSHOP $$
Bookstore founded in 1977, where students, scholars, and artists meet. A selection of subversive books—cultural theory, graphic arts, poetry, cinema...
136 E 3rd St., New York, NY 10009. Subway: F to 2 Av.

❷ ST. MARK'S COMICS $$
The temple to American comic books.
11 St. Marks Pl., New York, NY 10003. Subway: 6 to Astor Pl.

❸ WESTSIDER RARE & USED BOOKS $$
A little shop with books and records and CDs from floor to ceiling.
2246 Broadway, New York, NY 10024. Subway: 1 to 79 St.

❹ RIZZOLI BOOKSTORE $$ ♥
Famed New York City bookstore in a beautiful setting, specializing in art, fashion, and design books.
1133 Broadway, New York, NY 10010. Subway: N,R to 23rd St.

❺ ALBERTINE $$
An elegant, yet cozy bookstore with a wonderful selection of French language books.
972 5th Ave., New York, NY 10075. Subway: 6 to 77 St.

❻ STRAND BOOKSTORE $
The most impressive used bookstore on the planet: 18.65 miles of stacks on three levels! Large collection of rare books.
828 Broadway, New York, NY 10003. Subway: 4, 5, 6, N, Q, R, L to 14 St.-Union Sq.

❼ NATIONAL ARTS CLUB $$$
Located in a mid-nineteenth-century brownstone, this art center organizes all sorts of literary events.
15 Gramercy Park S., New York, NY 10003. Subway: 6 to 23 St.

❽ BOOKS OF WONDER $$
The largest bookstore devoted to little New Yorkers. Readings and meetings with authors are regularly organized. An entire room is dedicated to the world of Oz, as imagined by L. Frank Baum.
18 W 18th St., New York, NY 10011. Subway: F to 14 St.

❾ SISTER'S UPTOWN BOOKSTORE $$
Specializes in African-American culture.
1942 Amsterdam Ave., New York, NY 10032. Subway: C to 155 St.

❿ MCNALLY JACKSON BOOKS $$
Wonderful independent bookstore. Numerous events (meetings with authors, writers, and poets) and a café for refreshments while reading.
52 Prince St., New York, NY 10012. Subway: N, R to Prince St.

⓫ NEW YORK SOCIETY LIBRARY
It's the oldest library in the city, created in 1754.
53 E 79th St., New York, NY 10075. Subway: 6 to 77 St.

⓬ THE MORGAN LIBRARY & MUSEUM
Its first director claimed that this library contained every book but the *Tables of the Law*. His museum presents an impressive collection: drawings by Michelangelo, Rembrandt, and Picasso; the Gutenberg Bible; manuscripts of Dickens, Poe, Twain, Steinbeck, and Wilde; and scores from Beethoven and Mozart.
225 Madison Ave., New York, NY 10016. Subway: 6 to 33 St.

⓭ KITCHEN ARTS & LETTERS $$$
A bookstore specialized in cookbooks from around the world.
1435 Lexington Ave., New York, NY 10128. Subway: 6 to 96 St.

⓮ THE POWERHOUSE ARENA $$
Vast loft converted into a bookstore-gallery, exhibition, and event space.
37 Main St., Brooklyn, NY 11201. Subway: F to York St.

⓯ NEW YORK PUBLIC LIBRARY ♥
Fine example of American Beaux-Arts style; one of the most extraordinary libraries in the world.
5th Ave. at 42nd St., New York, NY 10018. Subway: 7 to 5 Av.

puddle. She grew to be a most [9] re and wonderful prod ction of a tenement district, a pretty girl. None of the dirt of Rum Alley seemed to be in her veins. The philosophers up-stairs, down-stairs and on the same floor, puzzled over it. When a child, playing and fighting with gamins in the street, dirt disguised her. Attired in tatters and grime, she went unseen. There came a time, however, when the young men of the vicinity said: "Dat Johnson goil is a pu+y good looker." About this peri [13] her brother remarked to her: "Mag, I'll tell yeh dis! See? Yeh've edder got teh go teh hell or go teh work!" Whereupon s' [3] went to work, [11] ving the feminine aversion of [5] ng to hell. By a chance, she got position in an establishment where they made collars and cuffs. She received a stool and a machine in a room where sat twenty girls of various shades of yellow discontent.

She perched on the stool and treadled at her machine all day, turning out collars, the name of whose brand could be noted for its irrelevancy to anything in connection with collars. At night she returned home to her mother. Jimmie grew [15] re enough [12] to take the vague po ition of head of the family. As incumbent of that office, he [4] tumbled upstairs late at night, as his father had done before him. [8] [7] He reeled about the room, swearing at his relations [6] r went to sleep on the floor. The other had gradually arisen to that deg [2] e of fame that she could bandy wor [1] ith her acquaintances among t e police-justices. Court officials called her by her [10] rst name. When she appeared they pursued a course which had been theirs for months. They invariably grinned and cried out: "Hello, Mary, you here again?" Her grey head wagged in

ÉLISE GODMUSE

08 A BREATH OF FRESH AIR

Central Park serves as New York's lungs, a green rectangle cut out of the gray city, 842 acres of calm. There are a multitude of things to see and do: a chess match in the shade of the Upper East Side, jogging along the water's edge, sunbathing on the lawn of Sheep Meadow, or a pause at Strawberry Fields to pay tribute to John Lennon while humming "Revolution," "Help," or "Imagine."

❶ STATUE OF ALICE IN WONDERLAND IN CENTRAL PARK ♥
Since 1959 this sculpted group, created by José de Creeft, has been welcoming children who love to climb on Lewis Carroll's characters.
E 74th St., New York, NY 10021.
Subway: 6 to 77 St.

❷ CONSERVATORY WATER
Picnic at the water's edge while navigating a little remote-controlled sailboat.
E 72nd St., New York, NY 10021.
Subway: 6 to 77 St.

❸ WOLLMAN MEMORIAL RINK
A magical ice-skating rink on winter nights that transforms into a playground come summer.
830 5th Ave., New York, NY 10065.
Subway: N, Q, R to 5 Av.-59 St.

❹ BETHESDA TERRACE & BETHESDA FOUNTAIN ♥
A bit of freshness around the legendary fountain, with four cherubs created by the American sculptress Emma Stebbins in 1873.
Terrace Dr., New York, NY 10021.
Subway: B, C to 72 St.

❺ JACQUELINE KENNEDY ONASSIS RESERVOIR
A favorite spot of joggers. Admire the Manhattan skyscrapers from the largest body of water in the park.
Between 86th St. and 96th St., New York, NY 10128.
Subway: B, C to 96 St.

❻ CHESS & CHECKERS HOUSE
The meeting place for lovers of chess and checkers, but also of backgammon and dominos.
Center Dr., New York, NY 10019.
Subway: 6 to 68 St.-Hunter College

❼ CENTRAL PARK CAROUSEL
A merry-go-round for the little ones perched on one of fifty-seven wooden horses.
65th St. Transverse, New York, NY 10023. Subway: A, C, B, D, 1 to 59th St.-Columbus Circle

❽ THE LOEB BOATHOUSE $$$
For a boatride on the lake or bicycling around it.
E 72nd St., New York, NY 10021.
Subway: 6 to 77 St.

❾ RUMSEY PLAYFIELD
The site of the Central Park SummerStage festival where concerts, readings, and operas are held.
909 5 Ave., New York, NY 10021.
Subway: 6 to 77 St.

❿ THE RAMBLE
A wooded labyrinth, and a paradise for amateur ornithologists.
79th St. Traverse, New York, NY 10024.
Subway: 6 to 77 St.

⓫ SWEDISH COTTAGE MARIONETTE THEATER
Beautiful staging of children's tales in a little wooden house.
W 79th St., New York, NY 10023.
Subway: B, C to 81 St.-Museum of Natural History

⓬ SHAKESPEARE GARDEN
Stroll through a garden of trees mentioned in Shakespeare's works.
79th St. Transverse, New York, NY 10024. Subway: B, C to 81 St.-Museum of Natural History

⓭ STRAWBERRY FIELDS ♥
A rosette on the ground and a "Garden of Peace" in memory of John Lennon, who was murdered on the sidewalk across the street. Designed by landscape architect Bruce Kelly, the circular black-and-white mosaic bearing the inscription "Imagine" was inaugurated on October 9, 1985 in the presence of Yoko Ono. Fans regularly lay flowers there.
W 72nd St., New York, NY 10023.
Subway: B, C to 72 St.

⓮ SAFARI PLAYGROUND
The playground is decorated with hippopotomus sculptures by the artist Bob Cassilly.
W 91st St., New York, NY 10025.
Subway: B, C to 86 St.

⓯ SHEEP MEADOW
Frisbee games, improvised picnics, or sunbathing, with views of Lower West Side buildings above the trees.
65th St. Transverse, New York, NY 10023. Subway: B, C to 72 St.

AURÉLIE LEQUEUX

09 PARK LIFE

Since you sometimes get the impression that the sky has disappeared behind the skyscrapers in New York, it's important to know the places where you can breathe a little. From Sheep Meadow (the immense lawn in Central Park) to the cool grass of the most secret gardens of the outer boroughs, the city is only a memory... and its white noise gone with the wind.

❶ GREENACRE PARK ♥
One of the most charming "pocket parks" in New York; close to the UN and famous for its waterfall.
217 E 51st St., New York, NY 10022.
Subway: E, M, 6 to Lexington Av.–53 St.

❷ CONCRETE PLANT PARK
Industrial architecture takes pride of place in a park bordering the Bronx River.
Entrance at Bruckner Blvd, Bronx, NY 10472. Subway: 6 to Whitlock Av.

❸ WEST SIDE COMMUNITY GARDEN
Here, neighborhood residents can obtain a little plot for a vegetable garden.
142 W 89th St., New York, NY 10024.
Subway: 1 to 86 St.

❹ PETER DETMOLD PARK
A secret garden offering beautiful views of the East River.
454 E 51st St., New York, NY 10022.
Subway: E, M, 6 to Lexington Av.–53 St.

❺ MSGR. MCGOLRICK PARK
An ideal place to escape from the Brooklyn bustle, with the bonus of a farmer's market on Sundays.
Russell St. and Monitor St., between Nassau Ave. and Driggs Ave., Brooklyn, NY 11222. Subway: G to Nassau Av.

❻ KISSENA PARK
A glimpse at the peaceful family atmosphere of Queens.
Fresh Meadow Ln. and Kissena Blvd., between Oak Ave., Underhill, and Booth Memorial Ave., Flushing, NY 11358.
Subway: 7 to Flushing–Main St.

❼ GREENBELT CONSERVANCY
Panoramic views of New York. Certain scenes of the movie *The Godfather* were shot here.
700 Rockland Ave., Staten Island, NY 10314. Staten Island Railroad to Grant City stop.

❽ FORT TRYON PARK
A very pretty garden with a view of the Hudson, home to the Cloisters museum, and devoted to European medieval art.
1 Margaret Corbin Dr., New York, NY 10040. Subway: A to 190 St.

❾ TUDOR CITY GREENS
Slightly raised above street level, lovely, shady, and peaceful little parks surrounded by skyscrapers.
25 Tudor City Pl., New York, NY 10017.
Subway: 4, 5, 6, 7 to Grand Central–42 St.

❿ WAVE HILL
Located high up in the Bronx, beautiful gardens overlooking the Hudson.
W 249th St. and Independence Ave., Bronx, NY 10471.
MetroNorth to Riverdale stop

⓫ 6BC GARDEN
A little garden in the heart of the East Village neighborhood where residents meet up. Summer events include horticultural and scientific classes and workshops, festivals, and performances.
6th St. between Aves B and C, New York, NY 10009.
Subway: 6 to 2 Av.

⓬ GARDEN AT THE CHURCH OF SAINT LUKE IN THE FIELDS
Located behind the church walls, a ravishing garden crisscrossed by little red-brick paths.
487 Hudson St., New York, NY 10014.
Subway: 1 to Christopher St.–Sheridan Sq.

⓭ PROSPECT PARK ♥
A 585-acre park with a wilder look than Central Park, designed by the same architects.
450 Flatbush Ave., Brooklyn, NY 11225.
Subway: B, Q, then S to Prospect Park

⓮ BROOKLYN BOTANIC GARDEN $
Several types of garden are planted here: fragrance garden, Japanese garden... Over 10,000 different plants spread over a 52-acre space, the majority blossoming between March and June.
990 Washington Ave., Brooklyn, NY 11225. Subway: 2, 3, 4 to Franklin Av.

⓯ CENTRAL PARK ♥
It took about twenty years and 20,000 workers to lay out this park designed by architects Frederick Olmsted and Calvert Vaux, and it opened to the public by parcels starting in 1858. It is the largest and busiest park in the city, a veritable haven of greenery surrounded by tall buildings. It contains numerous lawns, several artificial lakes, walking paths, two open-air ice-skating rinks, and a wilder area where birds come for refuge.
W 59th–110th Sts, between 5th Ave. and Central Park West. New York, NY.
Subway: 1 to 59 St.–Columbus Circle; N, Q, R to 5 Av–59 St.; B, C to 72 St. through 110 St. stops; 6 to 59 St. through 110 St. stops

SOPHIE LEDESMA

10 FEATHERS, SCALES, AND FUR

Domestic animals make up a significant segment of the New York population, the number of cats and dogs being estimated at 1.1 million. As a result, pet boutiques, bakeries, and even spas can be found throughout the city. To see animals of a more exotic variety, check out one of the zoos located in each borough.

1 CENTRAL PARK ZOO $$
Featured in the film *Madagascar*; over 130 animal species are present. You can watch the sea lions being fed, observe reptiles in the tropical rain forest, or admire the penguins and polar bears.
64th St. & 5th Ave., New York, NY 10021. Subway: N, Q, R to 5 Av.-59 St.

2 BRONX ZOO $$ ♥
One of the largest urban zoos in the world: 264 acres, 650 species, and over 6,000 animals in semi-liberty. There's a monorail to discover Asian wildlife, a jungle, and Congo gorilla forest… More interesting in summer, especially in June, when births occur.
2300 Southern Blvd., Bronx, NY 10460. Subway: 2, 5 to Bronx Park East

3 NEW YORK AQUARIUM ♥
A tribute to sharks, sea turtles, and sea lions.
602 Surf Ave., Brooklyn, NY 11224 Subway: F, Q to W 8 St.-NY Aquarium

4 PROSPECT PARK ZOO $
Kangaroos in Brooklyn.
450 Flatbush Ave., Brooklyn, NY 11225. Subway: B, Q to Prospect Park then switch to the S shuttle.

5 QUEENS ZOO $
Home to some 400 animals from around the world.
51-53 111th St., Corona, NY 11368. Subway: 7 to 111 St.

6 THE BARKING ZOO $$$
Finally, we know where to find organic pet chow! Store specializing in quality dog and cat foods, and a wide choice of wool or cotton doggy sweaters.
172 9th Ave., New York, NY 10011. Subway: C, E to 23 St.

7 CANINE STYLES $$$$
The right place for unearthing every dog's necessities: food, toys, clothes, bags, collars, beds, etc. Two canine ready-to-wear collections each year for dapper dogs.
830 Lexington Ave., New York, NY 10065. Subway: F to Lexington Av./63 St.

8 MUDDY PAWS $$
Groom Rex without breaking the bank; self-service.
447 Graham Ave., Brooklyn, NY 11211. Subway: L to Graham Av.

9 KIKI'S PET SPA & BOUTIQUE $$
A spa for pets who like to be pampered; also offers daycare and boarding.
239 Dekalb Ave., Brooklyn, NY 11205. Subway: J, M, Z to Marcy Av.

10 PS9 PET SUPPLIES $$
Pet toys galore. Beds, bags, bowls and food for cats and dogs.
169 N 9th St., Brooklyn, NY 11211. Subway: L to Bedford Av.

11 NEW YORK DOG SPA AND HOTEL $$$
Care and relaxation for man's best friend. And yes, dogs also need to unwind!
32 W 25th St., New York, NY 10010. Subway: N, R to 23 St.

12 LOVE THY PET $$ ♥
Very useful advice, a friendly welcome and a wide choice of products to spoil your dog, cat, or canary if they've been good.
164 Union St., Brooklyn, NY 11231. Subway: F, G to Carroll St.

13 BALTO STATUE
A tribute to the dog who crossed the tundra to bring medicine to children.
East Dr. at 67th St., New York, NY 10022. Subway: 6 to 68 St.-Hunter College

14 CLEMENTINE BAKERY $
A bakery that also caters to health-conscious dogs with organic biscuits.
299 Greene Ave., Brooklyn, NY 11238. Subway: G to Classon Av.

15 SPRINKLES $$
Cupcakes for dogs and their masters.
780 Lexington Ave., New York, NY 10065. Subway: N, Q, R, 4, 5, 6 to Lexington Av.-59 St.

GWENDAL LE BEC

11 HIDDEN PLEASURES

Visiting New York means throwing yourself into the constant agitation of an overcharged megapolis, becoming a part of the comings and goings of a gigantic anthill. Fortunately, if you are overcome by fatigue and have the urge to escape from this hectic race, there are quiet places hidden in the heart of the city: tea salons, private clubs, scenic routes, and peaceful bars. Here, finally, you can catch your breath in these well-hidden paradises.

❶ ATTABOY $$$
Discreet music, cozy atmosphere, and excellent cocktails.
134 Eldridge St., New York, NY 10002.
Subway: B, D to Grand St.

❷ THE RAINES LAW ROOM $$$
Soft lighting, candles…
Call the waiter by pressing a button.
48 W 17th St., New York, NY 10011.
Subway: F, M to 14 St.

❸ POETS HOUSE
Settle into an armchair, read poetry, and enjoy the view.
10 River Terrace, New York, NY 10282.
Subway: 1, 2, 3 to Chambers St.

❹ CIRCLE LINE SIGHTSEEING CRUISES $$
See a new perspective of the city on one of these cruises around Manhattan.
Pier 83, W 42nd St. and 12th Ave., NY 10036. Bus: M50 or M42 to 42nd St & 12th Ave.

❺ THE NOGUCHI MUSEUM $
Abstract sculptures, a Japanese garden and zen ambiance.
9-01 33rd Rd, Long Island City (Queens), NY 11106. Subway: N, Q to Broadway

❻ THE KING COLE SALON (AT ST REGIS HOTEL) $$$$ ♥
Thick carpeting, leather armchairs, and quiet conversations punctuated by the clinking of ice cubes in whiskey glasses.
2 E 55th St., New York, NY 10022.
Subway: E, M to 5 Av.-53 St.

❼ BURP CASTLE NYC $$ ♥
Whispering required. One word a bit too loud will earn you a severe "shhhh!" from the bartender.
41 E 7th St., New York, NY 10003.
Subway: 6 to Astor Pl.

❽ NEW YORK INSIGHT
Tibetan meditation center in a large loft with red-brick walls.
28 W 27th St., 10th floor, New York, NY 10001. Subway: N, R to 28 St.

❾ WEST VILLAGE
A quiet neighborhood that feels like a small European town.
In the rectangle formed by the Hudson River, W Houston St., 6th Ave. and W 14th St., New York, NY 10014.
Subway: 14 St.

❿ BROOKLYN HEIGHTS
Rows of red sandstone houses, shady streets, and Olympian calm.
In the rectangle formed by the Promenade, Atlantic Ave., Court St. and Cadman Plaza W., Brooklyn, NY 11201.
Subway: N, R to Court St.

⓫ MEDITATION ROOM (AT UNITED NATIONS)
A silent empty room; an altar of dark stones. The walls prevent the transmission of waves: no telephone or Wi-Fi.
480 E 42nd St., New York, NY 10017.
Subway: 4, 5, 6, 7, S to Grand Central-42 St.

⓬ THE WATER TABLE (AT INDIA STREET PIER) $$$$
Have a romantic dinner on the *Revolution*, a US Navy ship converted into a floating restaurant, during a 2.5-hour cruise on the East River.
10 India St., Brooklyn, NY 11222.
Subway: G to Greenpoint Av.

⓭ THE CARNEGIE CLUB $$$
A whiskey and cigar at the bar. The orchestra plays Sinatra's greatest hits.
156 W 56th St., New York, NY 10019.
Subway: N, Q, R to 57 St.-7 Av.

⓮ STATEN ISLAND FERRY ♥
Free ride around the New York Bay, and an unimpeded view of the Statue of Liberty.
Staten Island Ferry Whitehall Terminal, 4 S St., New York, NY 10004.
Subway: 1 to South Ferry

⓯ CHINESE SCHOLAR'S GARDEN
Pagoda, bamboo, and a replica of the garden of the city of Suzhou in China.
1000 Richmond Terrace, Staten Island, NY 10301. Take Staten Island Ferry to St. George Terminal, then S44 bus to Lafayette Av/Fillmore St.

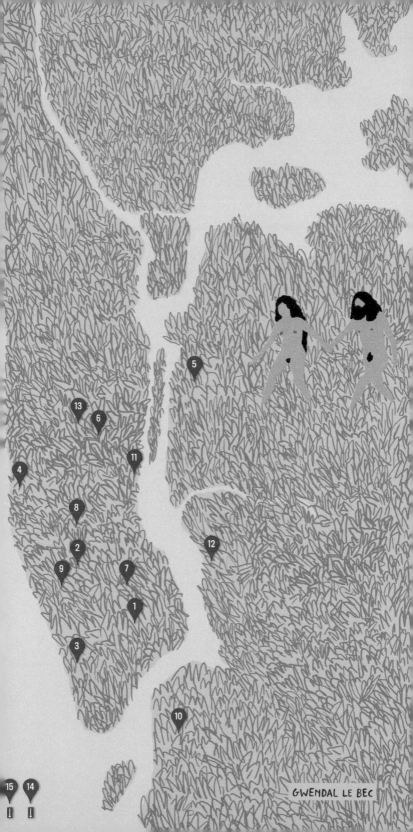

GWENDAL LE BEC

12 LAST STOP, CEMETERIES

New York's history is stippled on the headstones of its cemeteries. Take a silent and contemplative walk among the tombstones, family vaults and anonymous graves. Along the alleyways: the recumbent testimony of an upright city.

1 AFRICAN BURIAL GROUND NATIONAL MONUMENT (IN TED WEISS FEDERAL BUILDING)
According to historians, more than 15,000 African slaves were buried in mass graves on this site in the eighteenth century.
290 Broadway, New York, NY 10007. Subway: 1, 2, 3 to Chambers St.

2 GREEN-WOOD CEMETERY ♥
Inspired by the Père Lachaise Cemetery in Paris. It was *the* place to be buried in the second half of the nineteenth century.
500 25th St., Brooklyn, NY 11232. Subway: R to 25 St.

3 MORAVIAN CEMETERY
The oldest tombs date back to the middle of the eighteenth century.
2205 Richmond Road, Staten Island, NY 10306. Staten Island Railroad to Grant City

4 TRINITY CHURCH CEMETERY
Many important figures are buried here, including the naturalist Jean-Jacques Audubon, Alfred Tennyson Dickens (son of the writer Charles Dickens), and the wealthy John Jacob Astor, who died during the sinking of the *Titanic*.
770 Riverside Dr., New York, NY 10032. Subway: 1 to 157 St.

5 HARTSDALE PET CEMETERY ♥
Opened in 1896 and somewhat out of the city, it's the oldest pet cemetery in America.
100 N Washington Ave., Hartsdale, NY 10530. MetroNorth to Hartsdale

6 WOODLAWN CEMETERY
One of the largest cemeteries in New York—and a bit of countryside in the Bronx. Many mausoleums are interesting architectually, and for the famous people found there, including jazzmen and writers.
517 E 233rd St., Bronx, NY 10470. Subway: 4 to Woodlawn

7 NEW YORK CITY MARBLE CEMETERY
A very old cemetery dating from 1831, and somewhat private: an appointment is required for days they are not open to the public (917-780-2893).
52-74 E 2nd St., New York, NY 10003. Subway: F to 2 Av.

8 EAST COAST MEMORIAL
At the southern end of Manhattan, two steps from Wall Street.
Battery Park Underpass. Subway: R to Whitehall St.

9 FIRST SHEARITH ISRAEL GRAVEYARD
This small cemetery near Chatham Sq. served as the graveyard for the first Jewish settlers in North America in 1656.
55-57 St. James Pl., New York, NY 10038. Subway: J, Z to Chambers St.

10 NEW YORK MARBLE CEMETERY
Its design was unique: rather than coffins buried in the ground and topped by gravestones, family vaults were buried nine feet under due to sanitation concerns. Their locations are indicated by marble tablets set into the cemetery walls.
41 1/2 2nd Ave., New York, NY 10003. Subway: F to 2 Av.

11 CANARSIE CEMETERY
The space is shared by Catholic crosses, Stars of David, and steles paying tribute to soldiers who fell during the Civil War. Many graves of Italian immigrants are found here.
1370 Remsen Ave., Brooklyn, NY 11236. Subway: L to Canarsie–Rockaway Pkwy.

12 CALVARY CEMETERY
One of the largest and oldest cemeteries in the United States. Located in Queens, it gives a low-angle view over Manhattan.
4902 Laurel Hill Blvd, Woodside, NY 11377. Subway: 7 to 46 St.

13 MACHPELAH CEMETERY
Master escape artist Harry Houdini is buried here, in what is considered by some to be one of the creepiest graveyards in the city.
82-30 Cypress Hills Street, Ridgewood (Queens), NY, 11385. Subway: M to Fresh Pond Rd.

14 EVERGREENS CEMETERY ♥
Graves on the gently sloping hills and meadows among thousands of trees and flowering bushes.
1629 Bushwick Ave., Brooklyn, NY 11207. Subway: L to Bushwick Av.–Aberdeen St.

15 CYPRESS HILLS NATIONAL CEMETERY
The only national cemetery in New York; soldiers and civilians are buried here.
833 Jamaica Ave., Brooklyn, NY 11208. Subway: J to Cypress Hills

MIGUEL PORLAN

13 SACRED SPACES

Catholic, Methodist, Buddhist, Episcopalian, Jewish, Baptist ... Places of worship are numerous, and their locations are often closely linked to the history of the immigrants who were the first to settle there. Small or immense, they boast somewhat eclectic styles and now often seem to be a bit lost in the middle of the big city.

① TRINITY CHURCH
A charming neo-Gothic Episcopalian church at the end of Wall St., the third on this site.
75 Broadway, New York, NY 10006.
Subway: 4, 5 to Wall St.

② JOHN STREET CHURCH
This is where a slave sexton bought his freedom and founded the first black Methodist congregation in the country. The present building dates from 1841.
44 John St., New York, NY 10038.
Subway: 2, 3, A, C to Fulton St.

③ ST. PAUL'S CHAPEL
This Trinity Church annex houses a memorial to the victims of September 11.
209 Broadway, New York, NY 10007.
Subway: E to World Trade Center

④ THE CHURCH OF THE TRANSFIGURATION
A Gothic-revival church where the Episcopal Actors' Guild was founded, whose members included Charlton Heston and Joan Fontaine.
The characters in some of the stained-glass windows have actors' faces.
1 E 29th St., New York, NY 10016.
Subway: N, R, 6 to 28 St.

⑤ EASTERN STATES BUDDHIST TEMPLE
Come here to admire a hundred golden Buddhas illuminated by candles.
64 Mott St., New York, NY 10013.
Subway: 1, A, C, E, J, N, Q, R, Z, 6 to Canal St.

⑥ ISLAMIC CULTURAL CENTER OF NEW YORK
The largest mosque in the city.
1711 3rd Ave., New York, NY 10029.
Subway: 6 to 96 St.

⑦ THE BASILICA OF ST. PATRICK'S OLD CATHEDRAL ♥
The oldest cathedral in New York (1815); located in Little Italy, it is especially attended by Italians.
263 Mulberry St., New York, NY 10012.
Subway: 6 to Prince St.

⑧ MUSEUM AT ELDRIDGE ST.
Neo-moorish-style synagogue where scientist Jonas Salk was once a member.
12 Eldridge St., New York, NY 10002.
Subway: F to East Broadway

⑨ CHURCH OF THE INCARNATION
Known especially for its Art Nouveau stained-glass windows by William Morris and Louis Comfort Tiffany.
209 Madison Ave., New York, NY 10016.
Subway: 6 to 33 St.

⑩ ST. PATRICK'S CATHEDRAL
One of the world's largest cathedrals whose neo-Gothic style contrasts with the skyscrapers surrounding it.
5th Ave. and 50th St., New York, NY 10022. Subway: E, M to 5 Av.–53 St.

⑪ CONGREGATION SHEARITH ISRAEL SYNAGOGUE
Built in 1897 for the oldest Jewish congregation in New York.
8 W 70th St., New York, NY 10023.
Subway: B, C to 72 St.

⑫ THE CATHEDRAL CHURCH OF SAINT JOHN THE DIVINE ♥
Construction started on this Episcopalean cathedral in 1892, and it still is not finished. Each year, on the first Sunday of October, you can have your animals blessed, and from mid- to late-April, it's your bicycle's turn.
1047 Amsterdam Ave., New York, NY 10025. Subway: 1 to Cathedral Pkwy.

⑬ ABYSSINIAN BAPTIST CHURCH
Its most famous pastor, Adam Clayton Powell Jr. (1908–1972), a major figure in the battle against segregation, was the first New York African-American to be elected to Congress.
132 W 138th St., New York, NY 10030.
Subway: 2, 3 to 135 St.

⑭ MARBLE COLLEGIATE CHURCH ♥
The oldest Protestant congregation of New York.
1 W 29th St., New York, NY 10001.
Subway: N, R to 28 St.

⑮ ANGEL ORENSANZ FOUNDATION
Housed in the oldest Gothic-revival synagogue in New York, it has since been converted into an art gallery and performance space.
172 Norfolk St., New York, NY 10002.
Subway: F, M, J, Z to Essex St.

CHRISTIAN ROUX

14 NEW YORK PANORAMA

New York has no lack of dizzying points of view: helicopter rides, panoramic terraces, suspended gardens, and gigantic skyscrapers. Forget your vertigo and climb to the clouds, rise above it all, and discover the city as seen from the sky!

❶ AKA CENTRAL PARK $$$
Camp out with a giant telescope on the seventeenth-floor balcony of a five-star room to admire the sky.
42 W 58th St., New York, NY 10019.
Subway: N, Q, R to 5 Av.–59 St.

❷ ROOSEVELT ISLAND TRAMWAY
View over Manhattan, Queens, and the East River for the price of a tramway ticket.
59th St. and 2nd Ave, New York, NY 10044. Subway: N, Q, R to Lexington Av.–59th St.

❸ HOTEL ON RIVINGTON $$$
Rooms with panoramic bay windows, for a breathtaking way to wake up.
107 Rivington St., New York, NY 10002.
Subway: F to Delancey St.

❹ NEW YORK MARRIOTT MARQUIS $$$$
Enjoy a cocktail at revolving restaurant The View, with a magical 360° view over Manhattan.
1535 Broadway, New York, NY 10036.
Subway: N, Q, R to 49 St.

❺ BAR 54 (AT HYATT TIMES SQUARE) $$$ ♥
Fine wine on the 54th floor, overlooking the bright lights of Times Square.
135 W 45th St., New York, NY 10036.
Subway: N, Q, R to 49 St.

❻ EMPIRE STATE BUILDING ♥
A unique 360° panorama of the entire city.
350 5th Ave., New York, NY 10118.
Subway: B, D, F, M, N, Q, R to 34 St.-Herald Sq.

❼ TOP OF THE ROCK
Extraordinary terrace of the Rockefeller Center, with a superb view over Manhattan and Central Park.
30 Rockefeller Plaza, New York, NY 10112. Subway: B, D, F, M to 47-50 Sts- Rockefeller Center

❽ THE HIGH LINE
Walk along the suspended garden and admire the urban landscape of the West Village and Chelsea.
From Gansevoort St. and Washington St. to W 34th St. between 10th and 12th Avs. Subway: A, C, E, L to 14 St / 8 Av.

❾ GARDEN CAFÉ AND MARTINI BAR (AT THE MET) $$
In Central Park; come for the view of the skyline around the park. Sculptures on the roof.
1000 5th Ave., #5, New York, NY 10028.
Subway: 4, 5, 6 to 86 St.

❿ MANDARIN ORIENTAL, NEW YORK $$$$
A peaceful view over Central Park and the roofs of New York.
80 Columbus Circle, New York, NY 10023. Subway: A, C, B, D, 1 to 59 St.–Columbus Circle

⓫ ONE WORLD OBSERVATORY (AT ONE WORLD TRADE CENTER) ♥
Panoramic platform from the 100th floor of One World Trade Center, at over 1,776 ft. high!
285 Fulton St., New York, NY 10006.
Subway: E to World Trade Center

⓬ JIMMY (AT THE JAMES NEW YORK HOTEL) $$$
Outdoor terrace that juts out like a figurehead, with the Hudson and the new World Trade Center in the line of sight.
27 Grand St., New York, NY 10013.
Subway: 1 to Canal St.

⓭ TOP OF THE STANDARD (AT THE STANDARD HIGH LINE HOTEL) $$$
Very hip bar-restaurant perched on the eighteenth floor; breathtaking view.
848 Washington St., New York, NY 10014. Subway: A, C, E, L to 8 Av.

⓮ MANHATTAN HELICOPTERS
Break the piggy bank and fly over Manhattan by helicopter. Aircrafts take off from the downtown Manhattan heliport.
6 East River Piers, New York, NY 10004.
Subway: 1 to South Ferry

⓯ 230 FIFTH
Immense and cool terrace for taking in the Midtown skyscrapers.
230 5th Ave., New York, NY 10001.
Subway: N, R to 28 St.

XAVIER BARRADE

15 SPECTACULAR SELFIES

You've made your way to the Big Apple—now let the whole world know about it! Smile at the top of the Statue of Liberty, wink in Grand Central, stretch your arms out to the lights of Times Square. It's the thing to do, and it's hard to keep track of the number of initiatives from museums and cultural centers that celebrate the photographer's face next to a work of art. The Museum Selfie Day perfectly illustrates this phenomenon. This initiative, launched on Twitter by an international group of professionals from the art world, permits selfie addicts to take photos of themselves in front of an artwork and post it with hashtag #museumselfie. So break out your selfie stick and start snapping!

❶ TOP OF THE ROCK ♥
Go to the 70th floor of Rockefeller Center for a dizzying selfie.
30 Rockefeller Plaza, New York, NY 10111. Subway: B, D, F, M to 47–50 Sts–Rockefeller Center

❷ THE HIGH LINE ♥
1.3 miles of landscaped walkway for a bucolic selfie.
From Gansevoort St. and Washington St. to W 34th St. between 10th and 12th Avs. Subway: A, C, E, L to 23 St.

❸ TKTS TIMES SQUARE STAIRS
In the heart of Manhattan, for a selfie in the crowd.
1564 Broadway, New York, NY 10036. Subway: N, Q, R to 49 St.

❹ *LOVE* SCULPTURE BY ROBERT INDIANA
An unmissable artwork for a love-ly selfie.
1359 Ave. of the Americas, New York, NY 10019. Subway: F to 57 St.

❺ SKY ROOM (IN THE NEW MUSEUM)
Sleek design and 360° view for a selfie on the rooftops.
235 Bowery, New York, NY 10002. Subway: F to 2nd Av; J, Z to Bowery

❻ CIRCLE LINE SIGHTSEEING CRUISES (AT PIER 83)
Sunset cruise for a nautical selfie.
W 42nd St., New York, NY 10036. Subway: A, C, E to 42 St.–Port Authority Bus Terminal

❼ DUMBO WALLS: MOMO ♥
A hypercolored fresco for a street art selfie.
York St., Brooklyn, NY 11201. Subway: F to York St.

❽ BROOKLYN BRIDGE
Perch over the East River for a sunset selfie.
Brooklyn Bridge, New York, NY 10038 Subway: 4, 5, 6, to Brooklyn Bridge–City Hall

❾ GANTRY PLAZA STATE PARK
Take your place facing the Manhattan skyline for a panoramic selfie.
474 48th Ave., Long Island City, NY 11109.
Subway: 7 to Vernon Blvd.–Jackson Av.

❿ GRAND ARMY PLAZA
At the crossroads of Central Park and 5th Ave. for a chic selfie.
Grand Army Plaza, New York, NY 10019. Subway: N, Q, R to 5 Av.–59 St.

⓫ STATUE OF LIBERTY (ON LIBERTY ISLAND)
Stand under the skirts of Liberty for a symbolic selfie.
Board at Battery Park, 75 Battery Pl., New York, NY 10280.

⓬ ELLIS ISLAND
Walk in the footsteps of American immigration for a historic selfie.
Jersey City, NY 07305.
Access by boat via Liberty Island

⓭ ROOSEVELT ISLAND TRAMWAY
Rise 250 feet above ground for a suspended selfie.
Main St., Roosevelt Island, NY 10044. Subway: F to Roosevelt Island

⓮ EMPIRE STATE BUILDING
Go to the top of an iconic building for a classic New York selfie.
350 5th Ave., New York, NY 10118. Subway: B, D, F, M, N, Q, R to 34 St.–Herald Sq.

⓯ DOYERS ST.
Take a selfie on this legendary corner of Chinatown, where you can capture the vibrant energy of the neighborhood.
New York, NY 10013. Subway: 1, A, C, E, J, N, Q, R, Z, 6 to Canal St.

16 LOVE STORY

Promoted after decades of Hollywood movies, New York has become a leading destination for lovers from around the world. Kisses under the clouds, romantic dinners or moonlit walks, there are no cameras here—only eyes lost in those of your lover's, the silence of a gaze or the promise of a scene where no one will say, "Cut!"

❶ CARRIAGE RIDE IN CENTRAL PARK ♥
Go for a romantic ride, like in Woody Allen's *Manhattan*.
Central Park, from 59th St. to 110th St., from 5th Ave. to 8th Ave.
Departure from the Grand Army Plaza, at the southeast corner of Central Park.
Subway: N, Q, R to 5 Av.–59 St.

❷ THE RIVER CAFÉ $$$$
Under the Brooklyn Bridge, you can have a dinner along with a breathtaking view of Manhattan.
1 Water St., Brooklyn, NY 11201.
Subway: A, C to High St.

❸ GALLOW GREEN (IN MCKITTRICK HOTEL) $$$
The picturesque charm of a bar perched on a Chelsea rooftop.
542 W 27th St., New York, NY 10001.
Subway: 1 to 28 St.

❹ BOHEMIAN $$$
A restaurant hidden at the end of a hallway, in a NoHo building that once belonged to Andy Warhol and where the American painter Jean-Michel Basquiat had both his studio and home in the 1980s. A private place, its telephone number is shared among friends, but can be reached by e-mail through playearth.jp.
57 Great Jones St., New York, NY 10012.
Subway: B, D, F, M, 6 to Bleecker St.

❺ FLÛTE MIDTOWN $$$
A discreet and romantic champagne bar in a former speakeasy once run by the famous singer and actress, Texas Guinan. Intimate atmosphere with subtle lighting, a cocktail menu, and private rooms.
205 W 54th St., New York, NY 10019.
Subway: B, D, E to 7 Av.

❻ THE LOEB BOATHOUSE CENTRAL PARK $$$
A pastoral restaurant for nature lovers, located by the lake in Central Park.
E 72nd St., New York, NY 10021.
Subway: 6 to 77 St.

❼ CONEY ISLAND BEACH AND BOARDWALK ♥
Running the length of the beach, this boardwalk makes for a romantic stroll.
Surf Ave. and Stillwell Ave., Brooklyn, NY 11224. Subway: D, F, N, Q to Coney Island–Stillwell Av.

❽ MANHATTAN BY SAIL $$$
Wine-tasting on the *Shearwater* sailboat at sunset.
N Cove Marina, New York, NY 10281.
Subway: 1, N, R to Cortlandt St.

❾ WINTER VILLAGE (IN BRYANT PARK)
Ice-skate hand in hand in a Midtown French-style park.
41 W 40th St., New York, NY 10018.
Subway: 7 to 5 Av.

❿ GRAND CENTRAL OYSTER BAR & RESTAURANT $$$
Have the largest seafood selection before a final salty kiss on the platform.
89 E 42nd St., New York, NY 10017.
Subway: 4, 5, 6, 7 to Grand Central-42 St.

⓫ VINEGAR HILL HOUSE $$$
A country restaurant in Brooklyn, in the rustic and historic district on the seaside. Quiet garden and cherry trees in nice weather.
72 Hudson Ave., Brooklyn, NY 11201.
Subway: F to York St.

⓬ THE SPA AT TRUMP SOHO (IN TRUMP HOTEL) $$$$
Peaceful, luxurious, and spacious, it offers well-being rituals from around the world, with indoor and outdoor relaxation lounges, saunas, and private steam rooms in a Turkish decor.
246 Spring St., New York, NY 10013.
Subway: C, E to Spring St.

⓭ MAISON PREMIÈRE $$$ ♥
Champagne, white wine, and a beautiful replica absinthe fountain for a memorable evening. Also offers up to 30 types of oysters, depending on what's at the market.
298 Bedford Ave., Brooklyn, NY 11211.
Subway: L to Bedford Av.

⓮ NITEHAWK CINEMA $$ ♥
A fusion between bar and cinema, with double seats for lovers.
136 Metropolitan Ave., Brooklyn, NY 11249. Subway: L to Bedford Av.

⓯ CLASSIC HARBOR LINE (AT PIER 62) $$$
Take a boat ride to watch the sun set behind the Statue of Liberty.
Chelsea Piers, New York, NY 10011.
Subway: C, E to 23 St.

MARIE ASSÉNAT

coney island

17 SEX IN THE CITY

Under its geometric and cold exterior, New York hides a subversive and sulphurous subculture and it is even a pioneering American city in the matter. So there is no lack of sexy places, whether for an impromptu afternoon tryst, to pick up glamorous lingerie, or to watch a languorous striptease.

1 MUSEUM OF SEX $$
The first erotic museum in the United States. Exhibitions, conferences, and publications on the history and cultural evolution of sexuality. Permanent collection of over 15,000 objects, and a sizzling gift shop.
233 5th Ave., New York, NY 10016.
Subway: N, R, to 28 St.

2 FLASHDANCERS $$$
A famous striptease club.
1674 Broadway, New York, NY 10019.
Subway: B, D, E to 7 Av.

3 BABELAND $$
A famous temple for sex toys. The qualified staff offer expert advice and a wide variety of objects.
43 Mercer St., New York, NY 10013.
Subway: N, Q, R to Canal St.

4 LA PETITE COQUETTE $$
Lace, lingerie, high-quality swimwear, with exceptional prices during sales.
51 University Pl., New York, NY 10003. Subway: N, R to 8 St.–NYU

5 THE BOX $$$$
Dare to go to the lewd and provocative cabaret shows.
189 Chrystie St., New York, NY 10002.
Subway: F to 2 Av.

6 THE SLIPPER ROOM $$$ ♥
Laugh at the best burlesque shows in Manhattan.
167 Orchard St., New York, NY 10002.
Subway: F to 2 Av.

7 NURSE BETTIE $$
Cocktails, pinups, and burlesque shows.
106 Norfolk St., New York, NY 10002.
Subway: J, M, Z to Essex St.

8 NEW YORK BURLESQUE FESTIVAL $$
Glamour, glitter, striptease... A burlesque festival with international artists, which usually takes place the last week of September. Check ahead for dates. Information and reservations:
thenewyorkburlesquefestival.com

9 PLEASURE CHEST $$
A brand that has been around for 40 years, with stores in Los Angeles, Chicago, and New York. A very wide choice of sex toys and workshops to promote healthy sexuality. And, above all ... the heroines of *Sex and the City* shopped here.
156 7th Ave. S, New York, NY 10014.
Subway: 1, 2 to Christopher St.–Sheridan Sq.

10 HUNK-O-MANIA $$
Chippendales shows; ideal for a girls' night out.
301 W 39th St., New York, NY 10018.
Subway: N, Q, R, S, 1, 2, 3 to Times Sq.–42 St.

11 EVE'S GARDEN $$$
Tucked away on a building's twelfth floor, a temple of feminine pleasure; with a variety of books and erotic or sensual objects. Founded in 1974 by Dell Williams, a pioneer in the struggle for women's sexual freedom.
119 W 57th St., Suite 1201, New York, NY 10019. Subway: F to 57 St.

12 THE LEATHER MAN $$$
For men who like men in leather.
111 Christopher St., New York, NY 10014. Subway: 1 to Christopher St.–Sheridan Sq.

13 PINK PUSSYCAT BOUTIQUE $$
Accessorize your love life.
167 W 4th St., New York, NY 10014.
Subway: A, C, E, B, D, F, M to W 4 St.

14 KIKI DE MONTPARNASSE $$$$
A shop named after a sensual 1930s icon, the muse of numerous artists who gathered in the Montparnasse neighborhood of Paris. Delicate and sexy luxury lingerie, and panties embroidered with naughty words.
79 Greene St., New York, NY 10012.
Subway: N, R to Prince St.

15 THE ARTFUL BACHELORETTE $$$
White wine, champagne, and a nude male model (not bad at all!) for a girls' drawing class. Ideal for a bachelorette party. Mixed groups accepted.
Check website for information and reservations: theartfulbachelorette.com

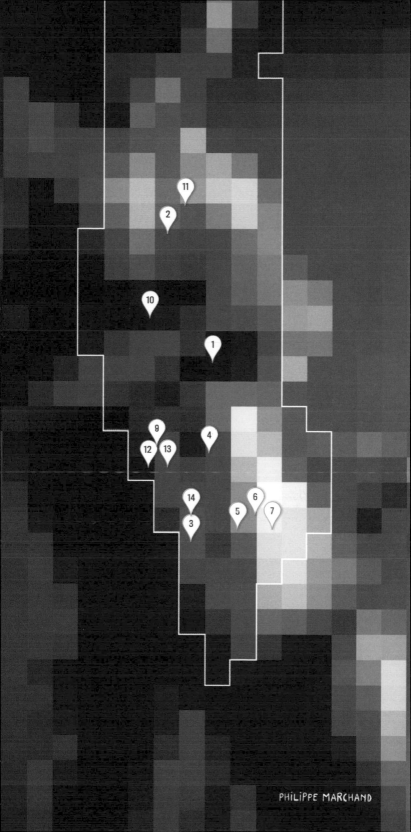

PHILIPPE MARCHAND

18 WHERE KIDS RULE

Endless avenues, dizzying skyscrapers, and the frantic pace of a city where there is always something happening. Add to that a candy store, a shop for superhero apprentices, a retro amusement park with an ocean view, and a mecca for videogamers, and you'll see why New York is the ideal destination for tots to teens.

1 ECONOMY CANDY $ ♥
Selling sweets at wholesale prices since 1930!
108 Rivington St., New York, NY 10002.
Subway: F, M, J, Z to Delancey St.

2 A NIGHT AT THE MUSEUM SLEEPOVER (AT THE AMERICAN MUSEUM OF NATURAL HISTORY) $$$
Discover the museum collections at night, for kids six to thirteen years old. Check in advance for dates and details.
Central Park W at W 79th St., New York, NY 10024. Subway: B, C to 81 St.–Museum of Natural History

3 VICTORIAN GARDENS AT WOLLMAN RINK (IN CENTRAL PARK) $
This family amusement park, only open in the summer, features twelve hand-crafted rides, games, and live interactive shows.
East side of Central Park between 62nd and 63rd Sts., New York, NY 10153.
Subway: N, Q, R to 5 Av.–59 St.; F to Lexington Av./63 St.

4 M&M'S WORLD $$
Three floors entirely devoted to the famous treats. All sorts of accessories to live the M&M's experience!
1600 Broadway, New York, NY 10019.
Subway: N, Q, R to 49 St.

5 BROOKLYN SUPERHERO SUPPLY CO. $$
A store devoted to superheroes: magic potions, capes…Profits are notably used to finance a writing workshop for disadvantaged neighborhood children.
372 5th Ave., Brooklyn, NY 11215.
Subway: R to 9 St.

6 NINTENDO WORLD (IN ROCKEFELLER CENTER) $$
The temple of the game console. There's space reserved for Pokémon, and the latest games for Nintendo Wii u and 3ds.
Rockefeller Center, 10 Rockefeller Plaza, New York, NY 10020.
Subway: B, D, F, M to 47-50 Sts–Rockefeller Center

7 THE LEGO STORE $$
The perfect place to let your imagination run wild while building with these famous little plastic bricks.
620 5th Ave. New York, NY 10020
Subway: B, D, F, M to 47-50 Sts–Rockefeller Center

8 MUSEUM OF THE MOVING IMAGE $
Discover the various steps that bring a film to life, from writing to directing, in this place devoted to the art, history, and technology of the moving image and cinema. Optical toys, exhibitions, educational programs, and screenings of classic and contemporary films from around the world.
36-01 35th Ave., Astoria, NY 11106.
Subway: M, R to Steinway St.

9 SONY WONDER TECHNOLOGY LAB
A free interactive museum to discover tomorrow's technologies.
550 Madison Ave., New York, NY 10022.
Subway: E, M to 5 Av.–53 St.

10 BROOKLYN CHILDREN'S MUSEUM ♥
Founded in 1899, this was the first museum in the world created expressly for children. 145 Brooklyn Ave., Brooklyn, NY 11213.
Subway: 3 to Kingston Av.

11 IMAGINATION PLAYGROUND
Giant construction sets, slides, and water activities in summer.
John St. and Front St., New York, NY 10038. Subway: 2, 3, A to Fulton St.

12 LUNA PARK IN CONEY ISLAND $$ ♥
Retro funfair, vintage rides, and an ocean view.
1000 Surf Ave., Brooklyn, NY 11224.
Subway: F, Q, to W 8 St.–NY Aquarium

13 CHILDREN'S MUSEUM OF MANHATTAN $
Educational and interactive activities for children.
212 W 83rd St., New York, NY 10024.
Subway: 1 to 86 St.

14 INTREPID SEA, AIR & SPACE MUSEUM (AT PIER 86) $$
Fans can visit an aircraft carrier and a submarine.
W 46th St. and 12th Ave., New York, NY 10036. Subway: A, C, E to 42 St.–Port Authority. Bus: M34 or M42 to 12th Ave. and Hudson River.

15 MADAME TUSSAUDS $$
Wax museum that continues to attract young and old, in spite of the endless waiting lines.
234 W 42nd St., New York, NY 10036.
Subway: 1, 2, 3 to Times Sq.–42 St.

19 SPORTY NEW YORK

New York is one of the few cities in the United States to not be too affected by the obesity epidemic that concerns so much of the country. The reason is simple: fanatical about eating healthy and organic foods, New Yorkers are also obsessed with sports! Basketball courts, baseball fields, swimming pools, and gyms— the exercise options are everywhere you look.

1 YANKEE STADIUM ♥
New York's most famous baseball stadium, entirely rebuilt in 2006 and reopened in 2009. Also hosts concerts and even football games.
1 E 161st St., Bronx, NY 10451.
Subway: B, D, 4 to 161 St.-
Yankee Stadium

2 MADISON SQ. GARDEN
Where to go to see a basketball or ice hockey game. Also hosts concerts, shows, and other events.
4 Pennsylvania Plaza, New York, NY 10001. Subway: A, C, E to 34 St.-Penn Station

3 HAMILTON FISH POOL
An outdoor Olympic-sized swimming pool on the Lower East Side. Free swimming classes during the summer.
128 Pitt St., New York, NY 10002.
Subway: F, M, J, Z to Essex St.

4 HIGHBRIDGE RECREATION CENTER
A newly renovated sports complex. Two outdoor swimming pools, dance room, gym, game room, baseball field, table tennis, and fitness room.
2301 Amsterdam Ave., New York, NY 10033. Subway: A, C to 168 St.

5 JOHN JAY SWIMMING POOL (IN JOHN JAY PARK)
Swimming pool on the edge of the East River.
77 Cherokee Pl., New York, NY 10075.
Subway: 6 to 77 St.

6 LASKER RINK (IN CENTRAL PARK)
A swimming pool in the summer, two ice-skating rinks in the winter: one for school hockey teams, the other for the public.
830 5th Ave., New York, NY 10065.
Subway: 2, 3 to Central Park North-110 St.)

7 CHELSEA PIERS SPORTS AND ENTERTAINMENT COMPLEX ♥
A luxurious sports center with an indoor pool. Many facilities, including a running track, training fields, and group and individual fitness classes.
60 Chelsea Piers, New York, NY 10011.
Subway: A, C, E, L to 14 St.

8 ASPHALT GREEN
The only indoor Olympic-sized pool in Manhattan. Water sports, for leisure or competition.
555 E 90th St., New York, NY 10128.
Subway: 4, 5, 6 to 86 St.

9 CHELSEA RECREATION CENTER
One of the largest sports centers in Manhattan. Volleyball, basketball, hockey, water polo, and computer and art classes.
430 W 25th St., New York, NY 10001.
Subway: C, E to 23 St.

10 RECREATION CENTER 54 ♥
One of the city's oldest sports centers built in 1911; it originally served as public baths intended for the working poor. It has bodybuilding, a basketball court, running track, and a swimming pool.
348 E 54th St., New York, NY 10022.
Subway: E, M, 6 to Lexington Av.-53 St.

11 GERTRUDE EDERLE RECREATION CENTER
Dozens of sports classes just steps from Columbus Circle. The center is named in honor of the American swimmer Gertrude Ederle, the first woman to swim across the English Channel on August 6, 1926, in 14 hours and 34 minutes.
232 W 60th St., New York, NY 10023.
Subway: 1 to 66 St.-Lincoln Center

12 ASSER LEVY RECREATION CENTER
These former public baths are now a sports complex firmly anchored in local community life. The historic building was designed by architects Arnold W. Brunner and William Martin Aiken.
392 Asser Levy Pl., New York, NY 10010. Subway: L to 1st Av.

13 HARLEM TAVERN $$
Immense sports bar for watching countless games.
2153 Frederick Douglass Blvd., New York, NY 10026.
Subway: 2, 3 to 116 St.

14 YANKEES CLUBHOUSE SHOP $$$
Dream gift shop for Yankees fans.
393 5th Ave., New York, NY 10016.
Subway: B, D, F, M, N, Q, R to 34 St.-Herald Sq.

15 NEW YORK RUNNING COMPANY
Shoes, advice, and sports equipment.
10 Columbus Circle, Time-Warner Center, 2nd fl., New York, NY 10019.
Subway: A, C, B, D, 1 to 59th St.-Columbus Circle.

MARINA DELRANC

20 PLAYFUL NEW YORK

New Yorkers are especially fond of outdoor games. Whether sports fields scattered around the city or magnificent playgrounds, these facilities are all highly prized by the locals, who come to take their minds off work on the weekends or at the end of the day.

❶ ST. NICHOLAS PARK
The park was designed in the early twentieth century by the architect Samuel Parsons Jr. One of the most popular basketball courts in Harlem, with handball courts, children's playground.
St. Nicholas Terrace, New York, NY 10027. Subway: B, C to 135 St.

❷ DE WITT CLINTON PARK ♥
The best basketball court in Midtown, along with baseball and football fields, and a handball court. Sports festival in August. Named after De Witt Clinton, a former mayor of New York City and a former governor of the state.
New York, NY 10019.
Subway: C, E to 50 St.

❸ HAPPY WARRIOR PLAYGROUND
Four mini basketball courts. This park owes its name to Alfred Emanuel Smith, who rose from the working class to be a four-time governor of the state of New York and was said by Franklin D. Roosevelt to be "the Happy Warrior of the political battlefield."
W 97th St. and Amsterdam Ave., New York, NY 10025.
Subway: 1, 2, 3 to 96 St.

❹ SARA ROOSEVELT PARK
Shaded basketball courts in the Lower East Side, with a soccer field, roller-skating rink, and playground.
From E Houston St. to Canal St., between Chrystie St. and Forsyth St., New York, NY 10002.
Subway: B, D to Grand St.

❺ WEST 4TH ST. COURTS
Boisterous basketball street games. "The Cage" hosts amateur tournaments.
Ave. of the Americas between W 3rd and W 4th Sts., New York, NY 10012.
Subway: A, C, E, B, D, F, M to W 4 St.

❻ MIDTOWN TENNIS CLUB
Chic tennis courts, opened since 1965; air-conditioned; private or group lessons.
341 8th Ave., New York, NY 10001.
Subway: 1 to 28 St.

❼ SUTTON EAST TENNIS
Play tennis a few steps from the Queensboro Bridge—eight clay courts installed under the bridge.
488 E 60th St., New York, NY 10022.
Subway: N, Q, R, 4, 5, 6 to Lexington Av. –59 St.

❽ ST. MARY'S PARK
The largest park in the south Bronx. The park also has basketball and handball courts and offers dance and swimming lessons.
450 St. Ann's Ave., Bronx, NY 10455.
Subway: 6 to E 143 St.–Saint Mary's St.

❾ CENTRAL PARK TENNIS CENTER
Twenty-six tennis courts right in the middle of Central Park.
New York, NY 10029.
Subway: B, C to 96 St.

❿ PIER 25 PLAY AREA
Has mini golf and beach volleyball; one of the nicest playgrounds in Manhattan.
225 West St., New York, NY 10013.
Subway: 1 to Franklin St.

⓫ PIER 6 PLAYGROUND (IN BROOKLYN BRIDGE PARK)
An immense playground in the heart of Brooklyn Heights.
Atlantic Ave. and Joralemon St., Brooklyn, NY 11201.
Subway: R to Court St.

⓬ ANCIENT PLAYGROUND
Inspired by the collection of Egyptian art at the Met, reconstructed in 2009 with a new set of stone tunnels and pyramids, wooden forts, an obelisk, and a sun dial. Bronze doors picturing Aesop's fables, designed in 1953 by Paul Manship, were removed from the park but have since been reinstalled.
E 85th St. and 5th Ave., New York, NY 10028. Subway: 4, 5, 6 to 86 St.

⓭ UNION SQ. PLAYGROUND ♥
Eccentric and offbeat. Has a shiny hemispherical dome, spirals to climb, and a rubber checkerboard surface.
E 16th St. and Park Ave. S, New York, NY 10003. Subway: L, N, Q, R, 4, 5, 6 to 14 St.–Union Sq.

⓮ RUCKER PARK
A legendary basketball court.
W 155th St. and 8th Ave., New York, NY 10039. Subway: B, D to 155 St.

⓯ ESPLANADE PLAZA
Wall St. workers play volleyball here after leaving the office.
Battery Park City, New York, NY 10280.
Subway: R to Rector St.

21 AMERICAN GRAFFITI

Art is everywhere in New York. It has left the museums and spilled onto the streets: tags, graffiti, and gigantic murals cover the brick walls of the world capital of street art. And while 5 Pointz, the graffiti mecca, has recently been demolished, other spots have already taken its place and continue the tradition of urban creation with style, color, and impertinence.

❶ MMUSEUMM
A minuscule museum of modern natural history—in an unmarked freight elevator in an alley—featuring contemporary objects that illustrate the complexity of today's world.
4 Cortlandt Alley, New York, NY 10013. Subway: J, Z to Canal St.

❷ *THE SPHERE*
Sculpture by Fritz Koenig that miraculously escaped the September 11 attacks. Then located by the Twin Towers in the World Trade Center, it has been transferred to Battery Park, with an eternal flame in memory of the victims.
Battery Park, New York, NY 10004. Subway: 4, 5 to Bowling Green

❸ *CRACK IS WACK* PLAYGROUND
Keith Haring's unmissable mural.
E 127th St., New York, NY 10035. Subway: F to 2nd Av.

❹ GRAFFITI HALL OF FAME
This immense wall running along the Metro-North line is a legend in the history of street art and has been constantly changing for thirty years.
E 106th St. and Park Ave., New York, NY 10029. Subway: 6 to 110 St.

❺ HOUSTON BOWERY WALL
The wall first painted by Keith Haring in 1982, and by many great graffiti artists since then.
E Houston St., New York, NY 10012. Subway: B, D, F, M, 6 to Bleecker St.

❻ SAILOR'S KISS ♥
Hypercolored reinterpretation by the artist Eduardo Kobra of the famous photo *V-J Day in Times Square*.
504 W 25th St., New York, NY 10001. Subway: C, E to 23 St.

❼ THE BUSHWICK COLLECTIVE
Striking murals in East Williamsburg. Damien Mitchell, Billy Mode, Chris Stain, Jef Aérosol…
St. Nicholas Ave. and Troutman St., New York, NY 11237.
Subway: L to Jefferson St.

❽ CENTRE-FUGE PUBLIC ART PROJECT
A shipping container transformed into an outdoor exhibition space.
E 1st St. between 2nd Ave. and Ave. A, New York, NY 10003. Subway: F to 2 Av.

❾ BERLIN WALL SEGMENTS
Works by two artists, French Thierry Noir and German Kiddy Citny, on this portion of the Berlin Wall, installed in Manhattan in 1990.
E 53rd St., New York, NY 10022. Subway: E, M to 5 Av.-53 St.

❿ TUFF CITY TATTOO $$$
A tattoo artist, a gallery, and a paradise for graffiti artists.
650 Fordham Rd., Bronx, NY 10458. Subway: B, D to Fordham Rd.

⓫ HUNTS POINT VILLAGE OF MURALS ♥
Committed, antisystem, activist, colorful murals.
Drake St. and Spofford Ave., Bronx, NY 10474. Subway: 6 to Longwood Av.

⓬ UNTITLED 2012
A 96 x 67 ft. mural created by the artist Barry McGee.
3 Lafayette Ave., Brooklyn, NY 11217. Subway: G to Fulton St.

⓭ 182 ALLEN ST.
Positioned way up high, a single work signed by WK Interact, a French street artist.
182 Allen St., New York, NY 10002. Subway: F to 2 Av.

⓮ GRAFFITI-STICKER MURAL (AT ACE HOTEL NEW YORK)
More than 40,000 stickers cover the walls of this hotel. It's the work of Bronx artist Michael Anderson.
20 W 29th St., New York, NY 10001. Subway: N, R to 28 St.

⓯ *BRANDON MANY RIBS* (AT HIGH LINE PARK)
The face of Brandon Many Ribs, a Native American Indian, member of the Lakota tribe, by the French artist JR.
W 29th St. and 30th St. at 10th Ave., New York, NY 10011. Subway: A, C, E to 34 St.

22 GANGS OF NEW YORK

At the end of 2014, the crime rate in New York City fell to the lowest level ever recorded. It was the end of a long road taken by the city that was once a symbol of crime and instability. Gang wars, settling scores, murders, assaults, the ever present mafia... The echo of this violent past still resonates in the dark alleys of the Bronx, Queens, Manhattan, and Brooklyn.

1 THE FIVE POINTS
The site of the gang wars immortalized in
Gangs of New York.
158 Worth St., New York, NY 10013.
Subway: J, Z to Chambers St.

2 DOYERS ST.'S BLOODY ANGLE
An alley set on fire and filled with blood
by Chinese gangs at the turn of the
twentieth century.
Doyers St., New York, NY 10013.
Subway: J, Z to Canal St.

3 HELL'S KITCHEN
The city's former skid row district.
In the rectangle formed by W 34th St. to
W 59th St. and 8th Ave. to the Hudson
River, New York, NY 10019.
Subway: C, E to 50 St.

4 21 BAXTER ST.
The meeting place of the Baxter St.
Dudes, a nineteenth-century teen gang.
New York, NY 10013.
Subway: 4, 5, 6 to Brooklyn Bridge–
City Hall

5 MUSEUM OF THE AMERICAN GANGSTER
Small crime museum located in a former
speakeasy.
80 St. Marks Pl., New York, NY 10003.
Subway: L to 1 Av.

6 TAMMANY HALL
The headquarters of a corrupt
nineteenth-century political organization.
100 E 17th St., New York, NY 10003.
Subway: N, Q, R, 4, 5, 6 to 14 St.–
Union Sq.

7 LA PLAZA CULTURAL
A former seedy corner transformed into
a community center.
The corner of 9th St. and Ave. C,
New York, NY 10009.
Subway: L to 1 Av.

8 PARK CENTRAL HOTEL NEW YORK
Arnold Rothstein was murdered in 1928
and Albert Anastasia in 1957 in this hotel
that was a Mafia hangout.
870 7th Ave., New York, NY 10019.
Subway: B, D, E to 7 Av.

9 UMBERTO'S CLAM HOUSE
One of the favorite restaurants of the
underworld, where Joey Gallo,
nicknamed "Crazy Joe," was killed on
April 7, 1972.
132 Mulberry St., New York, NY 10013.
Subway: 6 to Canal St.

10 RIVERSIDE PARK
The place where Beat generation writer
Lucien Carr killed David Kammerer on
August 14, 1944.
W 115th St., New York, NY 10024.
Subway: B, C to 116 St.

11 SPARKS STEAKHOUSE
Steakhouse where the infamous mob hit
of Gambino mob boss Paul Castellano,
ordered by John Gotti, took place
outside.
210 E. 46th St., New York, NY 10017.
Subway: 7 to Grand Central–42 St.

12 LANDMARK TAVERN
A former speakeasy during the
Prohibition Era, it was frequented by
gangster-turned-actor George Raft.
626 11th Ave, New York, NY 10036.
Subway: C, E to 50th St.

13 THE BOWERY
The headquarters of the Bowery Boys,
the legendary Five Points gang.
Bowery St., New York, NY 10012.
Subway: J, Z to Bowery

14 RAO'S
Founded in 1896, this super-exclusive
restaurant has seen bodies in suitcases
turn up down the block, and was the
infamous scene of the murder of
Albert Circelli.
455 East 114th St., New York, NY 10029.
Subway: 6 to 116 St.

15 BAMONTE'S
This former meeting place of the local
mafia is one of the recurring sets in
The Sopranos series.
32 Withers St., Brooklyn, NY 11211.
Subway: L to Lorimer St.

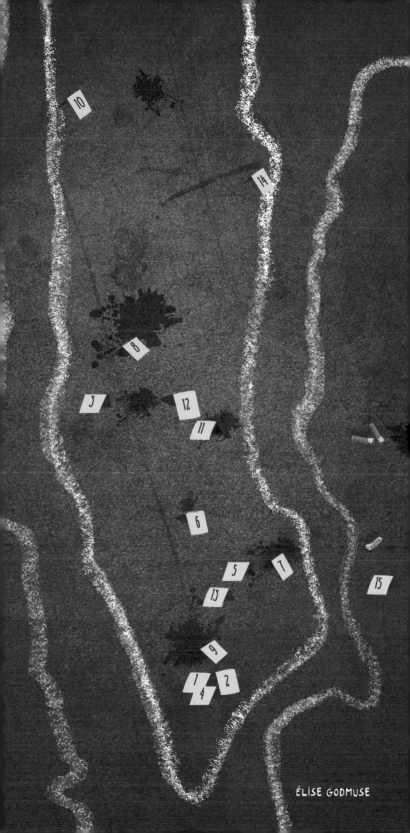

ÉLISE GODMUSE

23 SEEING STARS

Los Angeles–capital of movies, music, and glitter–is no longer the epicenter of the American star system. Today, celebrities are spending their free time in New York. Overpriced spas, bowling alleys, private clubs, gourmet restaurants, and hip pubs–between luxury and chic, discover the preferred spots of your favorite stars.

❶ LAFAYETTE GRAND CAFÉ & BAKERY $$$
Exceptional service in this French bistro frequented by Gwyneth Paltrow.
380 Lafayette St., New York, NY 10003.
Subway: 6 to Bleecker St.

❷ FORBIDDEN PLANET $$
A gigantic comic book store; Robin Williams was a regular customer.
832 Broadway, New York, NY 10003.
Subway: L to 14 St.–Union Sq.

❸ THE CARLYLE $$$$
Five-star hotel; Woody Allen's favorite New York address.
35 E 76th St., New York, NY 10021.
Subway: 6 to 77 St.

❹ BLUE HILL $$$$
Chef Dan Barber proposes a delicious and sophisticated cuisine, enjoyed by the likes of actor Edward Norton.
75 Washington Pl., New York, NY 10011.
Subway: A, C, E, B, D, F, M to W 4 St.

❺ NINTH ST. ESPRESSO $
In the words of Will Ferrell, "The world's best cup of coffee."
75 9th Ave., New York, NY 10011.
Subway: A, C, E to 14 St.

❻ WHAT GOES AROUND COMES AROUND $$$
A chic vintage store where Katy Perry and Mischa Barton shop.
351 W Broadway, New York, NY 10013.
Subway: A, C, E, 1 to Canal St.

❼ AVENUE $$$$
You have to be dressed to the nines to get through the door of this club and dance with Emma Watson, Fergie, or Rihanna.
116 10th Ave., New York, NY 10011.
Subway: A, C, E, L to 14 St.

❽ EQUINOX $$$
Bradley Cooper and Cameron Diaz's fitness club.
1 Park Ave., New York, NY 10016.
Subway: 6 to 33 St.

❾ INDOCHINE $$$
French-Vietnamese fusion food and celebrity spot popular with Sarah Jessica Parker, Kanye West, and Paris Hilton.
430 Lafayette St., New York, NY 10003.
Subway: 6 to Astor Pl.

❿ THE SPOTTED PIG $$$ ♥
The list of investors in this chic gastropub is impressive, including Jay-Z, Bono, and Michael Stipe.
314 W 11th St., New York, NY 10014.
Subway: 1 to Christopher St.–Sheridan Sq.

⓫ SERGE NORMANT $$$$
Hair salon and spa, the beauty secret of Julia Roberts and Sofia Vergara.
336 W 23rd St., New York, NY 10011.
Subway: C, E to 23 St.

⓬ LUCKY STRIKE MANHATTAN $$
The best bowling alley in the city.
Gerard Butler and Jim Carrey come here regularly to relax.
624–660 W 42nd St., New York, NY 10036. Subway: A, C, E to 42 St.–Port Authority Bus Terminal

⓭ GANSEVOORT MEATPACKING NYC $$$ ♥
Brad Pitt, Angelina Jolie, Leonardo DiCaprio, and Lindsay Lohan are aficionados of this ultra-celeb hotel.
18 9th Ave., New York, NY 10014.
Subway: A, C, E, L to 8 Av.

⓮ JEFFREY $$$$
A favorite shopping venue of Kim Kardashian.
449 W 14th St., New York, NY 10014.
Subway: A, C, E, L to 8 Av.

⓯ ABC KITCHEN $$$ ♥
Celebrities such as Jake Gyllenhaal and Meg Ryan come here from time to time to enjoy crab toast and house made ravioli.
35 E 18th St., New York, NY 10003.
Subway: 4, 5, 6, N, Q, R to 14 St.–Union Sq.

HILTON

GANGS OF NEW YORK

MAXIME GARCIA

24 MADE IN MANHATTAN (AND BROOKLYN)

New York is one of the largest movie sets in the world. It's a city filmed so often we have the impression of knowing it before even visiting it—a giant gorilla on the top of a skyscraper, a museum that comes to life at night, and a taxi driver with Ray-Bans and shaved head on the edge of madness. Go behind the scenes and take off in pursuit of New York cinema legends!

❶ GHOSTBUSTERS (AT HOOK & LADDER 8)
The headquarters from the film.
14 N Moore St., New York, NY 10013.
Subway: 1 to Franklin St.

❷ NIGHT AT THE MUSEUM (AT AMERICAN MUSEUM OF NATURAL HISTORY)
Search for the works seen in the film.
Central Park W and W 79th St.,
New York, NY 10024. Subway: C, B to
81 St.–Museum of Natural History

❸ BLACK SWAN (AT LINCOLN CENTER FOR THE PERFORMING ARTS)
Natalie Portman starred in this ballet at
Lincoln Center.
10 Lincoln Center Plaza, New York,
NY 10023. Subway: 1 to 66 St.–
Lincoln Center

❹ HAIR (IN CENTRAL PARK)
Hippies, the Bethesda Terrace arcades, a
love story…
Terrace Dr., New York, NY 10021.
Subway: B, C to 72 St.

❺ MADAGASCAR (IN CENTRAL PARK)
Alex the lion, Marty the zebra, Melman
the giraffe, and Gloria the hippopotamus—
heroes of the Central Park Zoo.
64th St. and 5th Ave., New York,
NY 10021. Subway: N, Q, R to 5 Av.–
59 St.

❻ BIRDMAN (IN ST. JAMES THEATER) ❤
It's in this theater that the character
played by Michael Keaton stages an
adaptation of a short story by
Raymond Carver.
246 W 44th St., New York, NY 10036.
Subway: A, C, E, N, Q, R, S, 1, 2, 3, 7 to
42 St.–Port Authority Bus Terminal

❼ MANHATTAN (IN SUTTON SQ.)
Woody Allen and Diane Keaton, filmed
from behind, seated on a bench facing
the Queensboro Bridge…
New York, NY 10022. Subway: E, M to
Lexington Av.–53 St.

❽ SATURDAY NIGHT FEVER
With bell-bottom pants and red-leather
shoes, John Travolta walks up the street
to "Stayin' Alive" by the Bee Gees.
Along 86th St., Brooklyn,
NY 11214. Subway: D to 20 Av.

❾ WEST SIDE STORY
The Jets and the Sharks clash on this
basketball court.
209 E 110th St., New York, NY 10029.
Subway: 6 to 110 St.

❿ ONCE UPON A TIME IN AMERICA
The heroes, still children, walk the streets
of Brooklyn, the Manhattan Bridge
closing the perspective between the red-
brick buildings…
Washington St. and Water St., Brooklyn,
NY 11201. Subway: F to York St.

⓫ BREAKFAST AT TIFFANY'S (AT TIFFANY & CO.)
The incomparable elegance of Audrey
Hepburn eating a croissant in front of a
Tiffany's window.
727 5th Ave., New York, NY 10022.
Subway: N, Q, R to 5 Av.–59 St.

⓬ KING KONG
The first appearance of the Empire State
Building in a movie, in 1933.
350 5th Ave., New York, NY 10118.
Subway: N, Q, R, B, D, F, M to 34 St.–
Herald Sq.

⓭ I AM LEGEND
This is where Dr. Robert Neville, played
by Will Smith, lives with his dog.
11 Washington Sq. N, New York,
NY 10003. Subway: A, C, E, B, D, F, M to
W 4 St.

⓮ TAXI DRIVER
Go here to relive the last violent scene of
the film Taxi Driver.
226 E 13th St., New York, NY 10003.
Subway: L to 3 Av.

⓯ MEN IN BLACK
The headquarters of MiB is located here.
Battery Pl., between Washington St.
and Greenwich St., New York,
NY 10004. Subway: 4, 5 to
Bowling Green

KANE

GLADYS GLOVER

JACK ROBIN
THE JAZZ SINGER

Singing in the Kitler

HELEN SINCLAIR
in
GOD OF OUR
FATHERS

GERITOL

DAILY BUGLE

GEKKO & CO.

BERNIE HOU

25 SOUL SINGERS

New York is one of the cities that offers a glimpse of some of the finest gospel music, spiritual songs that can be traced as far back as the seventeenth century. While some churches have become veritable tourist attractions, many have been able to preserve their authenticity and their fervor.

① ABYSSINIAN BAPTIST CHURCH ♥
The oldest African-American church in New York, founded in 1808, and probably the best-known Baptist church in the city. It's name is derived from "Abyssinia," the ancient name of the Ethiopian empire.
132 W 138th St., New York, NY 10030.
Subway: 2, 3 to 135 St.

② MOTHER AFRICAN METHODIST EPISCOPAL ZION CHURCH
Gospel music in the first church built by an African-American architect.
140-6 W 137th St., New York, NY 10030.
Subway: 2, 3 to 135 St.

③ CANAAN BAPTIST CHURCH OF CHRIST
Service renowned for the fervor of the singing. A historic church founded in 1932 by forty believers.
132 W 116th St., New York, NY 10026.
Subway: 2, 3, C, B to 116 St.

④ FIRST CORINTHIAN BAPTIST CHURCH
Long lines to attend Sunday services, where parishioners and tourists are seated separately. It's a large crowded church with passionate members.
1912 Adam Clayton Powell Jr. Blvd., New York, NY 10026. Subway: 2, 3, C, B to 116 St.

⑤ SALEM UNITED METHODIST CHURCH
An atmosphere emphasizing piety and the absence of ostentation. Simple beautiful songs, with a less crowded assemby than in other large churches.
2190 Adam Clayton Powell Jr. Blvd., New York, NY 10026. Subway: 2, 3, A, C, B, D to 125 St.

⑥ THE CONCORD BAPTIST CHURCH OF CHRIST
A far cry from the extravagance and pomp of Harlem churches, created in 1847 by four members of the Abyssinian Baptist Church, with gospel and jazz concerts.
833 Gardner C. Taylor Blvd., Brooklyn, NY 11216. Subway: A, C to Nostrand Av.

⑦ ST. CECILIA'S ROMAN CATHOLIC CHURCH
A red-brick church in the middle of the barrio of East Harlem. For 130 years the community has welcomed the faithful from many different countries. Services in English on Sunday, in English and Spanish the rest of the week.
120 E 106th St., New York, NY 10029.
Subway: 6 to 103 St.

⑧ BETHEL GOSPEL ASSEMBLY
A venerable community founded in 1917, which influences several churches in South Africa and sister churches in New Jersey, Virginia, Atlanta, and Florida.
2-26 E 120th St., New York, NY 10035.
Subway: 6 to 116 St.

⑨ TIMES SQ. CHURCH
Gospel services celebrated in a former theater: 8,000 people of 100 nationalites gather together each week in this immense church.
237 W 51st St., New York, NY 10019.
Subway: C, E, 1 to 50 St.

⑩ BROOKLYN TABERNACLE
This choir won six Grammy Awards. A vast auditorium, 10,000 faithful, and 250 choir members directed by Carol Cymbala, the pastor's wife, who also composes the music. Magnificent singing.
17 Smith St., Brooklyn, NY 11201.
Subway: A, C, F, R to Jay St.–MetroTech

⑪ THE CATHEDRAL CHURCH OF SAINT JOHN THE DIVINE ♥
Organ music and singing in one of the world's largest Christian churches.
1047 Amsterdam Ave., New York, NY 10025. Subway: 1 to 116 St.

⑫ THE MADISON AVENUE BAPTIST CHURCH
A choir of professional singers. The modern church, founded in 1848, transmits its faith with passion and humor. Podcasts of pastoral sermons can be downloaded from the Internet.
131 Madison Ave., New York, NY 10016.
Subway: 6 to 33 St.

⑬ METROPOLITAN COMMUNITY UNITED METHODIST CHURCH
An authentic church far from the tourist path.
1975 Madison Ave., New York, NY 10035. Subway: 4, 5, 6 to Harlem–125th St.

⑭ MIDDLE COLLEGIATE CHURCH
Singing, joy, and good cheer.
112 2nd Ave., New York, NY 10003.
Subway: 6 to Astor Pl.

⑮ FIRST PRESBYTERIAN CHURCH OF BROOKLYN
Songs influenced by jazz.
124 Henry St., Brooklyn, NY 11201.
Subway: 2, 3 to Clark St.

CHRISTIAN ROUX

26 COVERT NEW YORK

There is another New York, hidden behind the vertical facades of the postcard-perfect city–a discreet and unusual New York where one can play pinball while washing their clothes, or ride a tram in the sky to an island. In this secret New York, punk is not dead, magicians exist, and superheroes watch over the Big Apple.

❶ ARTHUR KILL SHIP GRAVEYARD
Boat cemetery sheltering forgotten giants of the sea.
Staten Island, NY 10309.
Staten Island Rail to Huguenot

❷ HALLOWEEN ADVENTURE $$
Crawling with all sorts of crazy costumes.
104 4th Ave., New York, NY 10003.
Subway: 6 to Astor Pl.

❸ SEARCH & DESTROY $$$
Shop for punk clothes to an angry punk-rock soundtrack.
25 St. Marks Pl., New York, NY 10003. Subway: 6 to Astor Pl.

❹ CHISHOLM LARSSON GALLERY $$$ ♥
Treat yourself to an original movie poster from their giant stock.
145 8th Ave., New York, NY 10011.
Subway: A, C, E, L to 14 St.

❺ ABRACADABRA $$$
Magic store with a wide variety of costumes and accessories.
19 W 21st St., New York, NY 10010.
Subway: N, R to 23rd St.

❻ THE BROOKLYN SUPERHERO SUPPLY CO. $$
Everything you need to be a superhero.
372 5th Ave., Brooklyn, NY 11215.
Subway: F, G, R to 9 St.

❼ RUSSIAN & TURKISH BATHS $$
The city's most authentic Turkish baths in the heart of the East Village.
268 E 10th St., New York, NY 10009.
Subway: L to 1 Av.

❽ THE CITY RELIQUARY ♥
A tiny atypical museum: abandoned dolls, a Statue of Liberty collection, and other curiosities.
370 Metropolitan Ave., Brooklyn, NY 11211. Subway: G to Metropolitan Av.

❾ ROOSEVELT ISLAND TRAMWAY
Climb aboard the Roosevelt Island Tramway, the city's only cable car.
Main St., Roosevelt Island, NY 10044.
Subway: F to Roosevelt Island

❿ CARLTON ARMS HOTEL $ ♥
A gem in the heart of Manhattan: skeleton in the lobby, murals, and strange objects. An amazing atmosphere! Various artists decorated the walls of the rooms. It's not luxurious, but is a very good value for a unique place.
160 E 25th St., New York, NY 10010.
Subway: 6 to 23 St.

⓫ SUNSHINE LAUNDROMAT AND CLEANERS $
To the right, a row of washing machines; to the left, a row of vintage pinball machines.
860 Manhattan Ave., Brooklyn, NY 11222. Subway: 6 to Greenpoint Av.

⓬ THE EVOLUTION STORE $$$
Skeletons, stuffed animals, and strange and terrifying objects...
120 Spring St., New York, NY 10012.
Subway: N, R to Prince St.

⓭ LENIN STATUE
Lenin on the Lower East Side.
250 E Houston St., New York, NY 10002. Subway: F to 2 Av.

⓮ TRINITY PLACE BAR & RESTAURANT $$
A bar-restaurant in a bank vault. It's a safe bet.
115 Broadway, New York, NY 10006.
Subway: 4, 5 to Wall St.

⓯ KENKA $$
A rather curious Japanese restaurant: turkey testicles, bull penis, and all the cotton candy you can eat. Traditional Japanese dishes are also available. Come early since it is often crowded.
25 St. Marks Pl., New York, NY 10003.
Subway: 6 to Astor Pl.

27 A CUT AND A SHAVE

Clearly more present on the other side of the Atlantic than in Europe, the barbershop is an institution in New York City. The red, white, and blue poles are a familiar and much-loved symbol of classic and retro-themed shops. Shaving soap, cream and brush, a straight razor and scissors are the tools that seduce both the young and the gray.

❶ MIDTOWN BARBERS (IN THE CHRYSLER BUILDING) $$
A barbershop redolent of the early twentieth century with its traditional black-and-white floor tiles.
405 Lexington Ave., New York, NY 10174. Subway: 4, 5, 6, 7, S to Grand Central–42 St.

❷ JOHN ALLAN'S $$$
The perfect place to visit for a dapper look before an important appointment. Luxury salons created in 1988 by John Allan, a former apprentice to the famous French hairstylist Jean Louis David.
611 5th Ave., New York, NY 10022. Subway: E, M to 5 Av.–53 St.

❸ PREMIUM BARBERSHOP $
A skilled staff for pampering, with magazines and flat screens for the wait.
299 E 52nd St., New York, NY 10022. Subway: E, M, 6 to Lexington Av.–51 St.

❹ NEIGHBORHOOD BARBER $
For a quick shave that follows the rules of the art, ask for Eric, who is recognized as one of the best barbers in town.
439 E 9th St., New York, NY 10009. Subway: L to 1 Av.

❺ FRANK'S CHOP SHOP $$
Young and qualified staff, with concierge services for the best customers.
19 Essex St., New York, NY 10002. Subway: F to East Broadway

❻ THE NEW YORK SHAVING COMPANY $$$
Pleasant ambiance and quality products for sale.
202 Elizabeth St., New York, NY 10012. Subway: J, Z to Bowery

❼ REAMIR & CO. BARBER SHOP $
A barbershop that has created its own line of products for men: shampoo, conditioner, hair gel, natural shaving cream, and aftershave with essential oils that are alcohol free with no artificial colors.
2587 Broadway, New York, NY 10025. Subway: 1, 2, 3 to 96 St.

❽ PAUL MOLÉ BARBERSHOP $
Old-world charm; the shop sign dates back nearly a century.
1034 Lexington Ave., New York, NY 10021. Subway: 6 to 77 St.

❾ IGOR'S CLEAN CUTS $
A classic shop with reasonable prices. Igor and his staff are very attentive.
20 1st Ave., New York, NY 10009. Subway: F to 2 Av.

❿ TOMCATS BARBERSHOP $ ♥
Here, a haircut comes with a beer.
130 India St., Brooklyn, NY 11222. Subway: G to Greenpoint Av.

⓫ EDDIE'S HAIRCUT & SHAVE $$
Traditional barber and hairdresser. A neighborhood place–locals, tourists, and policemen come here for a cut or a shave. Eddie's Shave Deluxe includes a face, head, and shoulder massage.
1295 1st Ave., New York, NY 10021. Subway: 6 to 68 St.–Hunter College

⓬ NEXT LEVEL BARBERSHOP $
Hot towels and individual TVs.
396 Broome St., New York, NY 10013. Subway: C, E to Spring St.

⓭ BARBER ROOM 306 $$
Old-school service for beards and mustaches.
306 Graham Ave., Brooklyn, NY 11211. Subway: L to Graham Av.

⓮ BLIND BARBER $$
Great barber and cocktail bar.
339 E 10th St., New York, NY 10009. Subway: L to 1 Av.

⓯ ELEGANT BARBERSHOP $
Music and barbers and stylists who listen.
310 4th St., Brooklyn, NY 11215. Subway: F, G, R to 9 St.

MARINA DELRANC

28 A GAY OLD TIME

New York has always been a key player in the history of the gay community. While for a long time it was confined to certain neighborhoods, like Chelsea or Greenwich Village, and more recently, Hell's Kitchen and Williamsburg in Brooklyn, gay culture is now present throughout the city: radio stations, TV channels, restaurants, shops… and even a church.

❶ GAY ST.
Charming little street that bore this name long before gays moved into the neighborhood.
New York, NY 10014. Subway: 1 to Christopher St.-Sheridan Sq.

❷ GAY LIBERATION
Admire George Segal's sculpture, a cherished symbol of the homosexual community.
W 4th St., New York, NY 10014. Subway: 1 to Christopher St.-Sheridan Sq.

❸ CUBBYHOLE $ ♥
A gay and lesbian bar decorated with umbrellas, stars, garlands, and kites. Your hetero friend is welcome.
281 W 12th St., New York, NY 10014. Subway: A, C, E, L to 8 Av.

❹ STONEWALL INN $ ♥
Gay bar raided by the police the night of June 28, 1969, setting off a series of riots that marked a turning point in the history of homosexual civil rights in the United States and the start of the LGBT movement. To commemorate this event, gay pride parades are organized in June all over the world.
53 Christopher St., New York, NY 10014. Subway: 1 to Christopher St.-Sheridan Sq.

❺ THE CATHEDRAL OF SAINT JOHN THE DIVINE
This cathedral, under construction since 1892 and still unfinished, is the largest cathedral in the world. Especially interesting for the causes it supports and the originality of its activities, it houses a memorial devoted to AIDS victims, next to which sits a basket filled with red ribbons inscribed with their first names.
1047 Amsterdam Ave., New York, NY 10025. Subway: 1 to 116 St.

❻ THE MONSTER $$
East Village institution: piano, shows, and dance floor.
80 Grove St., New York, NY 10014. Subway: 1 to Christopher St.-Sheridan Sq.

❼ INDUSTRY BAR $$
Industrial warehouse renovated into a pleasant bar with a chic design.
355 W 52nd St., New York, NY 10019. Subway: C, E to 50 St.

❽ NYC EAGLE BAR $$
Popular gay bar stretching over three floors, with a rooftop for enjoying hot dogs and hamburgers in summer. Leather is the look of choice.
554 W 28th St., New York, NY 10001. Subway: A, C, E, 1, 2, 3 to 34 St.-Penn Station

❾ HENRIETTA HUDSON $
An institution for lesbians and the gay friendly community. The bar is open 365 days a year.
438 Hudson St., New York, NY 10014. Subway: 1 to Houston St.

❿ METROPOLITAN $
Gay and lesbian bar patronized by a hip and arty crowd.
559 Lorimer St., Brooklyn, NY 11211. Subway: L to Lorimer St.

⓫ LIPS NYC $$
Restaurant, bar, and drag shows.
227 E 56th St., New York, NY 10022. Subway: 6, E, M to Lexington Av.-53 St.

⓬ CHELSEA MARKET $$
Market much loved by the locals, set up in a former cookie factory. Brick architecture, an 820-foot long hall, numerous vendors, and products.
75 9th Ave., New York, NY 10011. Subway: A, C, E, L to 14 St.

⓭ CHELSEA PINES INN $
Ambiance set by posters from the golden age of cinema throughout the five floors, with a concierge on call 24 hours a day. Rooms are comfortable in this gay and lesbian hotel where everyone is welcome.
317 W 14th St., New York, NY 10014. Subway: A, C, E, L to 8 Av.

⓮ CAFETERIA $$
Gay restaurant open twenty-four hours a day, seven days a week. Electric, modern, and intimate atmosphere.
119 7th Ave., New York, NY 10010. Subway: 1 to 18 St.

⓯ XES LOUNGE $$
Pleasant lounge bar, with karaoke twice a week.
157 W 24th St., New York, NY 10011. Subway: 1 to 23 St.

OLIVIER FONTVIEILLE

29 TATTOO CULTURE

Between the Bronx, Manhattan, Queens, and Brooklyn, there are more tattoo parlors than art galleries across New York. Spurred by the recent explosion of the hipster movement, passing under the ink gun has practically become a ritual for New York youth. In summer the streets of Williamsburg and Bushwick quickly look like a living exhibition: tribal arabesques, old-school swallows, or Chicano frescoes—here, art is skindeep!

❶ NEW YORK ADORNED $$$ ♥
Talented tattoo artists, friendly atmosphere, and pretty jewelry.
47 2nd Ave., New York, NY 10003.
Subway: F to 2 Av.

❷ THREE KINGS TATTOO $$
Artwork on the walls, a warm welcome and meticulous work to make each tattoo a unique creation.
572 Manhattan Ave., Brooklyn, NY 11222. Subway: G to Nassau Av.

❸ EAST RIVER TATTOO $$$
Gothic chandeliers, exposed beams, rough wood walls, and a gigantic wind rose on the floor of this famous Brooklyn parlor.
1047 Manhattan Ave., Brooklyn, NY 11222. Subway: G to Greenpoint Av.

❹ RED ROCKET TATTOO $$
One of the best parlors in Midtown where the artists are as friendly as they are talented.
78 W 36th St., New York, NY 10018.
Subway: N, Q, R, B, D, F, M to 34 St.–Herald Sq.

❺ INKSHOP TATTOO $$
Eric Rignall, tattoo artist since 1995, specializes in fine lines, detailed pieces and realistic motifs.
209 Ave. A, New York, NY 10009.
Subway: L to 1 Av.

❻ NORTH STAR TATTOO $$
Parlor specializing in more traditional styles, including Japanese Irezumi.
74 E 7th St., New York, NY 10003.
Subway: 6 to Astor Pl.

❼ EAST SIDE INK $$
Manhattan parlor whose clientele include the likes of Rihanna.
97 Ave. B, New York, NY 10009.
Subway: F to 2 Av.

❽ DAREDEVIL TATTOO $$
A world-famous parlor and a little tattoo museum.
141 Division St., New York, NY 10002.
Subway: F to East Broadway

❾ KINGS AVE. TATTOO $$
Without a doubt, Mike Rubendall is one of the world's top tattoo artists.
188 Bowery, New York, NY 10012.
Subway: J, Z to Bowery

❿ INVISIBLE NYC INC $$$
A tattoo parlor that doubles as an art gallery in the heart of New York.
148 Orchard St., New York, NY 10002.
Subway: F, J, M, Z to Delancey St.

⓫ HAND OF GLORY TATTOO $$
Artists specialized in tattoo flash in an intimate atmosphere.
429 7th Ave., Brooklyn, NY 11215.
Subway: F, G to 7 Av.

⓬ TATTOO CULTURE $$
Impressionist creations and unique motifs between abstract and figurative.
128 Roebling St., Brooklyn, NY 11211.
Subway: L to Lorimer St.

⓭ FLYRITE TATTOO $$ ♥
A renowned parlor open for over 15 years.
492 Metropolitan Ave., Brooklyn, NY 11211. Subway: L to Lorimer St.

⓮ SAVED TATTOO $$$
A favorite parlor of many Brooklyn artists.
426 Union Ave., Brooklyn, NY 11211.
Subway: L to Lorimer St.

⓯ RISING DRAGON TATTOOS $$
High-end equipment, eight passionate artists and reasonable prices.
51 W 14th St., Suite 2F, New York, NY 10011. Subway: L, F, M to 14 St.

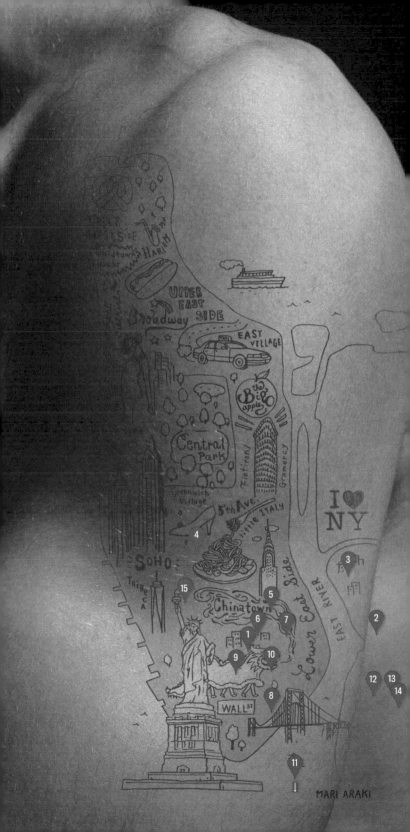

30 RECORD BREAKERS

Aim for the sky, fly beyond the clouds, reach the stars, and always think bigger. Gigantic stores, stellar skyscrapers, and astronomic spending: New York follows the rhythm of an ultracompetitive America, breaking record after record, in a frantic race to excess.

❶ CROWN BUILDING ♥
In 2014 the Spitzer family gave up 730 5th Ave. for the modest sum of 1.8 billion dollars, making the Crown Building the world's most expensive office building.
730 5th Ave., New York, NY 10119.
Subway: N, Q, R to 5 Av.–59 St.

❷ BROOKLYN GRANGE ROOFTOP FARM ♥
A vegetable garden on a Queens rooftop;, the largest of its kind in the world.
37-18 Northern Blvd., Long Island City, NY 11101. Subway: D, N, R to 36 St.

❸ NEW YORK BY GEHRY
Frank Gehry's design, with its crinkled and undulating metal facade, was finished in 2011, and for four years remained the tallest residential skyscraper in the western hemisphere.
8 Spruce St., New York, NY 10038.
Subway: A, C, J, Z, 2, 3, 4, 5 to Fulton St.

❹ 432 PARK AVENUE
Reaching 1,396 feet, this skyscraper, inaugurated in early 2015, is now the highest residential skyscraper in the western hemisphere.
New York, NY 10022.
Subway: E, M to 5 Av–53 St.

❺ KEW GARDENS HILLS
Ashrita Furman, holder of the largest number of Guinness World Records, grew up in this neighborhood.
Queens, NY 11367. Subway: E, F to Kew Gardens–Union Turnpike.

❻ CHRISTIE'S $$$$
On November 12, 2014, Christie's totaled the highest amount ever reached during an auction: 852.9 million dollars.
20 Rockefeller Plaza, New York, NY 10020.
Subway: B, D, F, M to 47-50 Sts-Rockefeller Center

❼ TOYS 'R' US $$
To make kids' dreams come true at the world's biggest toy store: 110,000 sq. ft..
1514 Broadway, New York, NY 10036.
Subway: A, C, E, 7, N, Q, R, 1, 2, 3, S to Times Sq.–42 St.

❽ THE NEW YORK TIMES BUILDING
In 2008, Alain Robert, the French "Spider-man," climbed the 748 ft. high glass surface to the roof of The New York Times Building.
620 8th Ave., New York, NY 10018.
Subway: A, C, E, 7, N, Q, R, 1, 2, 3, S to Times Square–42 St.

❾ NATHAN'S FAMOUS $
Hot-dog shack that hosts a contest each year of who can eat the most hot dogs.
1310 Surf Ave., Brooklyn, NY 11224.
Subway: D, F, N, Q to Coney Island–Stillwell Av.

❿ SERENDIPITY 3 $$
For 214 dollars, you can enjoy the Quintessential Grilled Cheese, the world's most expensive sandwich.
225 E 60th St., New York, NY 10022.
Subway: 4, 5, 6, N, Q, R to 59 St.

⓫ BROOKLYN BRIDGE
This iconic bridge, completed in 1883, was the longest suspension bridge in the world at the time, with a main span of 1,595 feet.
New York, NY 10007 Subway: 4, 5, 6 to Brooklyn Bridge–City Hall

⓬ ONE WORLD TRADE CENTER
This 1,792-foot-tall glass tower is the tallest skyscraper in the Western world.
285 Fulton St., New York, NY 10007.
Subway: A, C, E, 2, 3, E to World Trade Center

⓭ WYCKOFF HOUSE MUSEUM
Built in 1652, it's the oldest house in New York.
5816 Clarendon Rd., Brooklyn, NY 11203. Subway: L to Canarsie–Rockaway Pkwy.

⓮ TCS NEW YORK CITY MARATHON
The most-run marathon in the world; the first Sunday of every November. From Staten Island to Central Park by way of Brooklyn and Queens.

⓯ *THE PHANTOM OF THE OPERA* (AT THE MAJESTIC THEATER)
With nearly 12,000 performances since 1988, *The Phantom of the Opera* holds the record for longevity amongst Broadway shows.
247 W 44th St., New York, NY 10036.
Subway: A, C, E, 7, N, Q, R, 1, 2, 3, S, to 42 St.–Port Authority Bus Terminal

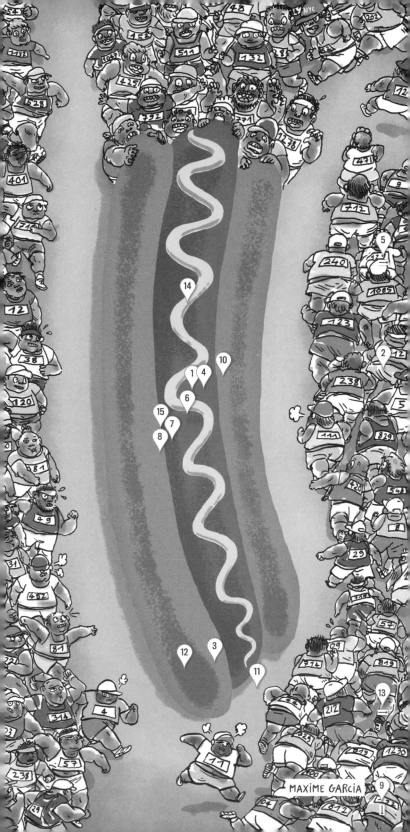

31 VINTAGE MANIA

New clothes are old hat. Here, vintage is a religion, and dressing secondhand is practically an obligation. Pop-up thrift shops on the streets of Williamsburg, weekly flea markets, 1970s jeans and grannie sweaters...Welcome to New York, paradise of the unique and a mecca for sartorial treasure hunters!

① NEW & ALMOST NEW $$
Carefully selected vintage clothing. This store, founded in 1995 by Maggie Chan, offers elegant and timely designer labels, shoes, bags, and accessories.
171 Mott St., New York, NY 10013.
Subway: J, Z to Bowery

② GOODWILL INDUSTRIES STORE AND DONATION CENTER $ ♥
One of the best-stocked thrift stores in the city.
2196 5th Ave., New York, NY 10037.
Subway: 2, 3 to 135 St.

③ GREENFLEA MARKET $$
One of the largest and oldest flea markets in New York City; held on Sundays in a school courtyard. You'll find antiques, vintage objects, collectibles, clothes, and refreshments.
100 W 77th St., New York, NY 10024.
Subway: C, B to 81 St.–Museum of Natural History

④ HELL'S KITCHEN FLEA MARKET $$ ♥
Operating since 1976, this is one of the city's most authentic flea markets.
W 39th St., New York, NY 10018.
Subway: 1, 2, 3, 7, N, Q, R, A, C, E, S to 42 St.–Port Authority Terminal

⑤ THE MARKET NYC $$ ♥
An opportunity to meet young designers and artisans at work. This vast, covered market–the largest retail store on historic Bleecker St.–notably offers clothing, vintage jewelry, art books, lamps, paintings, and handmade soap.
159 Bleecker St., New York, NY 10012.
Subway: 1 to Houston St.

⑥ CROSSROADS TRADING CO. $$
You can buy and sell in this shop, which offers lots of designer label clothing.
135 N 7th St., Brooklyn, NY 11211.
Subway: G to Bedford Av.

⑦ DSW (DESIGNER SHOE WAREHOUSE) $$
The paradise of shoe bargains.
40 E 14th St., New York, NY 10003.
Subway: N, Q, R, 4, 5, 6, L to 14 St.–Union Square

⑧ NORDSTROM RACK UNION SQUARE $$
Discounted items from Nordstrom department store.
60 E 14th St., New York, NY 10003.
Subway: N, Q, R, 4, 5, 6, L to 14 St.–Union Sq.

⑨ A SECOND CHANCE $$$
Uncover super-discounted vintage treasures or resell your own.
Among the finds are creations by Hermès, Chanel, and Louis Vuitton.
155 Prince St., New York, NY 10012.
Subway: C, E to Spring St.

⑩ CENTURY 21 $$
Very wide selection of discounted clothing.
22 Cortlandt St., New York, NY 10007.
Subway: Cortlandt St.
1972 Broadway, New York, NY 10023.
Subway: 1 to 66 St-Lincoln Center

⑪ MICHAEL'S, THE CONSIGNMENT SHOP FOR WOMEN $$$
Clothing left behind by stylish Upper East Side ladies.
1041 Madison Ave., New York, NY 10075. Subway: 1 to 77 St.

⑫ DAVE'S NEW YORK $$
The place to go for inexpensive Levi's in New York.
581 Ave. of the Americas, New York, NY 10011. Subway: L, F, M to 14 St.

⑬ NEW YORK VINTAGE $$$
The ultimate source for vintage couture.
117 W 25th St., New York, NY 10011.
Subway: F, M to 23 St.

⑭ PIPPIN VINTAGE JEWELRY $$
The best selection of vintage jewelry.
112 W 17th St., New York, NY 10011.
Subway: 1 to 18 St.

⑮ BROOKLYN FLEA $$
Paradise of bargain-hunters in search of a rare find.
Winter location:
241 W. 37th St., Brooklyn, NY 11232
Subway: D, N, R to 36 St.
Summer locations:
176 Lafayette Ave., Brooklyn, NY 11238.
Subway: C to Clinton–Washington Av.
and 50 Kent Ave., Brooklyn, NY
N 11th St. and N 12th St., Brooklyn,
NY 11211. Subway: G to Nassau Av.

GREYGOUAR

32 VINYL PLAY

Every purist will tell you: the audio perfection of electronic files will never replace the charm of vinyl records... Whether you're a curious LP lover or a collector looking for that rare find, if you love music head for these shops, veritable temples to "it was better before."

① BLACK GOLD RECORDS $$
Drink a cup of coffee and buy vintage records in a place with an offbeat decor.
461 Court St., Brooklyn, NY 11231.
Subway: F, G to Carroll St.

② ROUGH TRADE NYC $$
The famous British record shop in Brooklyn since 2013.
64 N 9th St., Brooklyn, NY 11249.
Subway: L to Bedford Av.

③ TURNTABLE LAB $$
Vinyl and hi-fi: a DJ's paradise.
120 E 7th St., New York, NY 10009.
Subway: L to 1 Av.

④ GENERATION RECORDS $$ ♥
Rare and precious albums.
210 Thompson St., New York, NY 10012.
Subway: N, R to 8 St.–NYU

⑤ NORMAN'S SOUND AND VISION $$
The best rock and vinyl records, some for only one dollar!
555 Metropolitan Ave., Brooklyn, NY 11211. Subway: L to Lorimer St.

⑥ OTHER MUSIC $$
Ultra-knowledgeable sales staff to help uncover hidden treasures; specialized in underground, original, and experimental music.
15 E 4th St., New York, NY 10003.
Subway: 6 to Astor Pl.

⑦ ACADEMY RECORDS & CDS $$ ♥
One of the best record stores in New York. Selling books since 1977, the store expanded in 1995 to also specialize in music and film.
12 W 18th St., New York, NY 10011.
Subway: N, Q, R, 4, 5, 6, L to 14 St.–Union Sq.

⑧ A1 RECORD SHOP $$
A record store for over 20 years. Soul, jazz, and hip-hop. You can listen in the store before buying.
439 E 6th St., New York, NY 10009.
Subway: F to 2 Av.

⑨ GOOD RECORDS NYC $$$
An East Village star since 2005, featuring a selection of music from Africa, Brazil, Latin America, and the Caribbean. Various styles include 1950s songs and current trends.
218 E 5th St., New York, NY 10003.
Subway: 6 to Astor Pl.

⑩ DEADLY DRAGON SOUND SYSTEM $$$
A temple of reggae in the heart of Chinatown. Recent Jamaican music, *mento*, ska, and Internet podcasts.
102 Forsyth St., New York, NY 10002.
Subway: B, D to Grand St.

⑪ HUMAN HEAD RECORDS $
A stock of over 5,000 CDs and vinyl records. Various styles of music and prices.
168 Johnson Ave., Brooklyn, NY 11206.
Subway: L to Montrose Av.

⑫ THE THING $
A true Aladdin's cave. Floor to ceiling vinyl records that owner Larry Fisher bought at auctions.
1001 Manhattan Ave., Brooklyn, NY 11222. Subway: G to Greenpoint Av.

⑬ CO-OP 87 RECORDS $$
A tiny shop filled with good music. Rock, soul, jazz, hip-hop, disco, but also calypso, traditional Irish music, and Bollywood.
87 Guernsey St., Brooklyn, NY 11222.
Subway: G to Nassau Av.

⑭ EARWAX RECORDS $$
An excellent selection of electronic music and hi-fi equipment: turntables, speakers, integrated amps...
167 N 9th St., Brooklyn, NY 11211.
Subway: L to Bedford Av.

⑮ HALCYON $$
A vast choice of underground music. Pastoral atmosphere: grass and pebbles on the floor, wood on the walls, and record bins.
57 Pearl St., Brooklyn, NY 11201.
Subway: F to York St.

33 A WORLD OF SHOPPING

Get off at Canal St. to experience Chinese culture, or 116th St. for Senegal, Brighton Beach for Russia, and Bowery for Italy. For international goods, a change of scenery, or exotic food and spices, New York's cultural wealth lets you travel without ever leaving the city, offering a world tour for the price of a subway ticket!

1 SOCKERBIT $
Meaning "sugarcube" in Swedish, this minimally designed candy shop features over 140 kinds of Scandinavian sweets.
89 Christopher St. New York, NY 10014. Subway: 1, 2 to Christopher St.-Sheridan Sq.

2 HUNG CHONG IMPORT $
A Chinese wholesaler for equipping your kitchen.
14 Bowery St., New York, NY 10013. Subway: F to East Broadway

3 CASA LATINA MUSIC SHOP $$$
Latin-American music treasure chest opened over 30 years ago.
151 E 116th St., New York, NY 10029. Subway: 6 to 116 St.

4 RAICES DOMINICANAS CIGARS $$
Hand-rolled cigars direct from the Dominican Republic.
2250 1st Ave., New York, NY 10029. Subway: 6 to 116 St.

5 MALCOLM SHABAZZ HARLEM MARKET $$
Market devoted to African crafts: textiles, hair braids, wooden statuettes, jewelry, dishes, and clothing for women, men and children. Sellers from Senegal, Nigeria, Kenya, and Ghana.
52 W 116th St., New York, NY 10026. Subway: 2, 3 to 116 St.

6 YARA AFRICAN FABRICS $
A huge selection of fabric and clothing imported from Africa: dyed, woven, brocaded, waxed, and batiks. It's possible to order made-to-measure outfits in various patterns and colors.
2 W 125th St., New York, NY 10027. Subway: 2, 3 to 125 St.

7 SURMA – THE UKRAINIAN SHOP $$
Crafts from the Ukraine: hand-painted eggs,fabric, kilims, porcelain, ceramics, embroidered shirts, books, and icons. The art of *pysanka*, or egg decorating, is a tradition that has existed in Ukraine for centuries. Legend has it that as long as this activity persists, the world will continue to exist.
11 E 7th St., New York, NY 10003. Subway: 6 to Astor Pl.

8 ALLEVA $$ ♥
Opened since 1892, this appetizing little shop is one of the last remains of Little Italy.
188 Grand St., New York, NY 10013. Subway: 6 to Spring St.

9 HONG KONG SUPERMARKET $
An Asian supermarket that is worth a visit, with signs and descriptions in the native language.
157 Hester St., New York, NY 10013. Subway: B, D to Grand St.

10 AJI ICHIBAN $
The specialist in candied exotic fruit and Japanese-style salty crackers.
37 Mott St., New York, NY 10013. Subway: J, Z to Canal St.

11 DEAN & DELUCA $$$ ♥
A SoHo institution in a magnificent building; lots of Italian products.
560 Broadway, New York, NY 10012. Subway: N, R to Prince St.

12 SUNRISE MART $
A superior-quality Japanese grocery store with an astonishing selection of fresh fish. Rare products, cold red-bean cakes, marshmallows, and gummies.
4 Stuyvesant St., 2nd fl., New York, NY 10003. Subway: 6 to Astor Pl.

13 KALUSTYAN'S $$ ♥
More than 4,000 varieties of herbs, spices, and exotic products.
123 Lexington Ave., New York, NY 10016. Subway: 6 to 28 St.

14 SAHADI'S $
Nuts, dried fruit, and Greek specialties.
187 Atlantic Ave., Brooklyn, NY 11201. Subway: 2, 3, 4, 5, R to Borough Hall

15 BANGKOK CENTER GROCERY $
Tiny store that offers a wide choice of Thai products and Asian specialties.
104 Mosco St., New York, NY 10013. Subway: 1, 2, 3 to Chambers St.

Casa Latina
MUSIC SHOP
RUBIO RECORDS DIST. CORP

ALLE-VA

Parmigiano Reggiano

良優の
HI BAN

HUNG CHONG IMPORT E INC.

MARION ALFANO

34 LUXE LIFE $$$$

If it's said that 5th Ave. is paved with gold, that's probably because it was—and still is—where multimillionaires and billionaires from around the world reside, but also because luxury stores follow each other without interruption, from Central Park to the Flatiron building. Department stores, jewelers, and high fashion, this culture of pricey and chic is not limited to the storefronts on the avenue, however: it radiates throughout the center of Manhattan.

❶ BLOOMINGDALE'S
Known for their iconic "little brown bag," Bloomingdale's has been a New York landmark since 1927, offering a wide selection of high-end designer clothing.
1000 3rd Ave. New York, NY 10022.
Subway: N, Q, R to Lexington Ave/59 St.

❷ TIFFANY & CO.
Jeweler turned institution, perhaps due to Audrey Hepburn's grace and charm.
727 5th Ave., New York, NY 10022.
Subway: N, Q, R to 5 Av.–59 St.

❸ TIME WARNER CENTER
Luxury shopping center graced within glass-clad architecture.
10 Columbus Circle, New York, NY 10019. Subway: A, C, B, D, 1 to 59 St.–Columbus Circle

❹ SAKS FIFTH AVENUE
Very chic, very traditional, and very expensive department store.
611 5th Ave., New York, NY 10022.
Subway: E, M to 5 Av–53 St.

❺ BARNEYS NEW YORK
A bit like Le Bon Marché in Paris, where all the top designers are on display.
660 Madison Ave., New York, NY 10065.
Subway: F to Lexington Av.–63 St.

❻ DE BEERS
Rubies, emeralds, and jewelry set with diamonds.
703 5th Ave., New York, NY 10022.
Subway: E, M to 5 Av–53 St.

❼ BERGDORF GOODMAN
Eight floors of the hottest designer collections.
754 5th Ave., New York, NY 10019.
Subway: N, Q, R to 5 Av.–59 St.

❽ HERMÈS MADISON
The famous label from Faubourg Saint-Honoré in Paris.
691 Madison Ave., New York, NY 10065.
Subway: F to Lexington Av.–63 St.

❾ GUCCI
One of the New York stores of the celebrated Italian firm founded in 1921.
725 5th Ave., New York, NY 10022.
Subway: E, M to 5 Av–53 St.

❿ LOUIS VUITTON NEW YORK
The initials of the famous trunk maker are now the signature of luxury leather goods.
611 5th Ave., New York, NY 10022.
Subway: N, Q, R to 5 Av.–59 St.

⓫ PRADA
An Italian label born in Milan; this location celebrated its centenary in 2013.
724 5th Ave., New York, NY 10019.
Subway: N, Q, R to 57 St.

⓬ CHANEL
To find the intertwined Cs of the famous label created by Coco Chanel.
15 E 57th St., New York, NY 10022.
Subway: N, Q, R to 5 Av.–59 St.

⓭ SALVATORE FERRAGAMO (IN THE TRUMP TOWER)
The early twentieth-century Florentine shoemaker that conquered the US market.
655 5th Ave., New York, NY 10022.
Subway: E, M to 5 Av–53 St.

⓮ DIOR
Experience the elegance of the designer who revolutionized postwar fashion with his New Look.
21 E 57th St., New York, NY 10022.
Subway: N, Q, R to 5 Av.–59 St.

⓯ MANOLO BLAHNIK ♥
Carrie Bradshaw's favorite designer in *Sex and the City*.
31 W 54th St., New York, NY 10019.
Subway: F to 57 St.

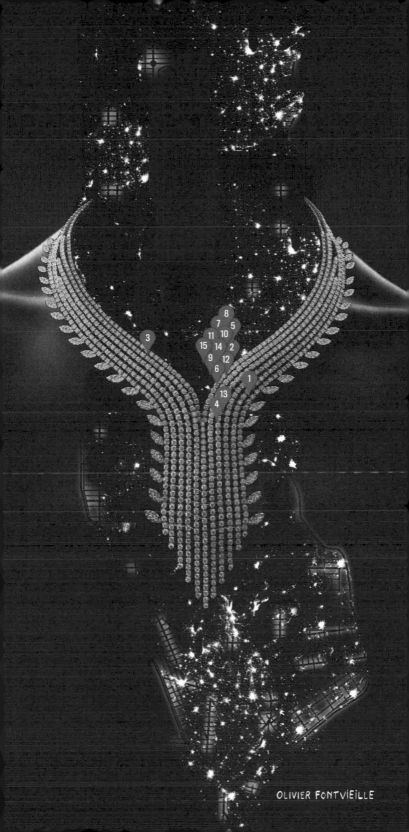

OLIVIER FONTVIEILLE

35 SUPER CHEFS

Stars here are not only on the American flag... they are also bestowed on some of the city's greatest restaurants. With over seventy starred establishments, New York prances at the head of the pack of Michelin's most awarded destinations and without a doubt wins the prize for culinary diversity. Japanese, Mexican, French, and international fusion–an unforgettable gastronomic journey awaits you, guided by the talent, inventiveness, and passion of chefs from around the world.

❶ PER SE $$$$ ♥
For its truffles and foie gras.
Chef: Thomas Keller.
10 Columbus Circle, New York, NY 10019.
Subway: N, Q, R to 57 St.-7 Av.

❷ LE BERNARDIN $$$
For its fish and seafood.
Chef: Éric Ripert.
155 W 51st St., New York, NY 10019.
Subway: 1 to 50 St.

❸ JEAN-GEORGES (IN TRUMP INTERNATIONAL HOTEL & TOWER) $$$
For French cuisine with pronounced Asian accents.
Chef: Jean-Georges Vongerichten.
1 Central Park W, New York, NY 10023.
Subway: A, C, B, D, 1 to 59 St.–Columbus Circle

❹ MASA $$$$ ♥
For its traditional Japanese cuisine.
Chef: Masayoshi Takayama.
10 Columbus Circle, New York, NY 10019. Subway: A, C, B, D, 1 to 59 St.–Columbus Circle

❺ DANIEL $$$
For its French cuisine inspired by the seasons.
Chef: Daniel Boulud.
60 E 65th St., New York, NY 10065.
Subway: 6 to 68 St.–Hunter College

❻ ELEVEN MADISON PARK $$$$
For its New York culinary traditions based on local products.
Chef: Daniel Humm.
11 Madison Ave., New York, NY 10010.
Subway: N, R to E 23 St.–Broadway

❼ CHEF'S TABLE AT BROOKLYN FARE $$$$
To savor fish and, especially, seafood.
Chef: Cesar Ramirez.
200 Schermerhorn St., Brooklyn, NY 11201. Subway: A, C, 6 to Hoyt-Schermerhorn Sts

❽ ATERA $$$
For revisited American cuisine that appeals to all the senses.
Chef: Ronny Emborg.
77 Worth St., New York, NY 10013.
Subway: 1 to Franklin St.

❾ BIANCA $$
For its Italian cuisine.
Chef: Carlo Mirarchi.
5 Bleecker St., New York, NY 10012.
Subway: 6 to Bleecker St.

❿ ICHIMURA AT BRUSHSTROKE $$$
For the best of sushi traditions.
Chef: Eiji Ichimura.
30 Hudson St., New York, NY 10013.
Subway: 1, 2, 3 to Chambers St.

⓫ AQUAVIT (IN PARK AVE. TOWER) $$$ ♥
For its Nordic cuisine. It's the first Nordic restaurant located in the heart of Manhattan.
Chef: Emma Bengtsson.
65 E 55th St., New York, NY 10022.
Subway: E, M to 5 Av–53 St.

⓬ JUNGSIK $$$
For its contemporary Korean cuisine.
Chef: Jung Sik Yim.
2 Harrison St., New York, NY 10013.
Subway: 1 to Franklin St.

⓭ THE MUSKET ROOM $$$
For its New Zealand-inspired cuisine. A menu where ancient local traditions mix with influences coming from Asia.
Chef: Matt Lambert.
265 Elizabeth St., New York, NY 10012.
Subway: 6 to Bleecker St.

⓮ CASA ENRIQUE $$
For its stellar Mexican cuisine. The first starred Mexican establishment.
Chef: Cosme Aguilar.
5-48 49th Ave., Long Island City, NY 11101.
Subway: 7 to Vernon Blvd.–Jackson Av.

⓯ M. WELLS STEAKHOUSE $$$
For its French-Canadian specialties.
Chef: Hugue Dufour.
43-15 Crescent St., Long Island City, NY 11101.
Subway: 7 to Court Sq.

MIGUEL MONTANER

36 LOCAL FLAVOR

Pizzas, hamburgers, hot dogs, bagels: the list of international specialties that the city has adopted is endless. If you're the least bit gourmand and not scared off by calories, you will always find a reason to enjoy a snack or an excuse to explore another New York restaurant.

① CUPPING ROOM CAFÉ $$
Traditional American cooking and atmosphere in the heart of SoHo.
359 W Broadway, New York, NY 10013.
Subway: A, C, E to Canal St.

② TRIBECA GRILL $$$
A typical New York grill, co-owned by Robert De Niro.
375 Greenwich St., New York, NY 10013.
Subway: A, C, E to Canal St.

③ KATZ'S DELICATESSEN $$ ◉ ♥
The oldest and most authentic of New York delis; it's also where the heroine of *When Harry Met Sally* staged an orgasm. Originally named Iceland Brothers when opened in 1888, the place was re-named in 1910 after Willy Katz, a Russian Jewish immigrant. You'll witness a loud and rowdy show in this genuinely family-run restaurant. The specialty: pastrami or corned-beef on rye bread with huge sour pickles.
205 E Houston St., New York, NY 10002. Subway: F to 2 Av.

④ SYLVIA'S RESTAURANT $$ ♥
The best place in New York for Southern soul food. This legendary Harlem restaurant is run by Sylvia Woods, dubbed the "Queen of Soul Food." You can come for weekend brunch which on Sunday includes live gospel music (by reservation).
328 Malcolm X Blvd., New York, NY 10027. Subway: 2, 3 to 125 St.

⑤ KITCHENETTE $$
Famous brunch at this cool and crowded restaurant in central Harlem.
1272 Amsterdam Ave., New York, NY 10027. Subway: 1 to 125 St.

⑥ CAFFÈ STORICO $$$
A renowned brunch or lunch in the very pretty Italian café at the New York Historical Society Museum & Library.
170 Central Park W, New York, NY 10024.
Subway: C, B to 81 St.–Museum of Natural History

⑦ UMAMI BURGER $$
Unforgettable, gourmet burgers in a casual setting.
432 6th Ave., New York, NY 10011.
Subway: A, C, E, B, D, F, M to W 4 St.

⑧ ESS-A-BAGEL $ ♥
A restaurant that doesn't look like much. And yet it has the best bagels in Manhattan.
831 3rd Ave., New York, NY 10022.
Subway: 51 St.

⑨ PETE'S TAVERN $$
Once a prohibition speakeasy, now known for its brunch and nightlife. This restaurant-bar, dating from 1864, has managed to keep its decor and atmosphere from yesteryear. Italian-American cuisine.
129 E 18th St., New York, NY 10003.
Subway: N, Q, R, 4, 5, 6, L to 14 St.–Union Square

⑩ PATSY'S $$
Located in Spanish Harlem; the tastiest pizzas in town are served here.
2287 1st Ave., New York, NY 10035.
Subway: 6 to 116 St.

⑪ JULIANA'S $$
In the shadow of two bridges, one of the best pizza crusts in New York.
19 Old Fulton St., Brooklyn, NY 11201.
Subway: A, C to High St.

⑫ FARA PIZZA $$
Here every pizza is unique, specially created for each customer!
1424 Ave. J, Brooklyn, NY 11230.
Subway: Q to Av. J

⑬ ABSOLUTE BAGELS $
Don't be put off by the mundane decor, the bagels here are delicious.
2788 Broadway, New York, NY 10025.
Subway: 1 to Cathedral Parkway

⑭ BAREBURGER $$
A recent mini-chain of gourmet organic burgers in a green-themed decor that is all the rage.
535 LaGuardia Pl., New York, NY 10012.
Subway: 6 to Bleecker St.

⑮ LOMBARDI'S $$
The oldest pizzeria in New York (open since 1905), and one of the best.
32th Spring St., New York, NY 10012.
Subway: 6 to Spring St.

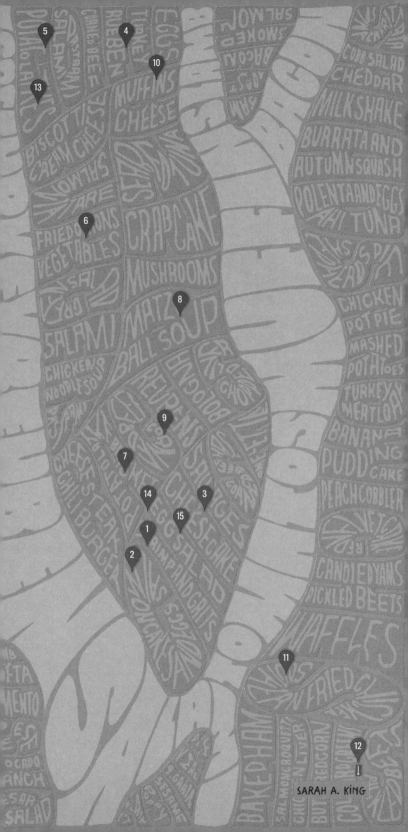

SARAH A. KING

37 THE BIG (ORGANIC) APPLE

Whether in search of rare spices for entertaining at home, organic bread and veggies for a casual picnic, or simply to snack on while out for a leisurely stroll: there are so many quality stores in New York that you'll find just what you're looking for in no time!

❶ TO THE WORLD FARM $
Vegetables, fruit, and other fresh produce.
655 Grand St., Brooklyn, NY 11211.
Subway: L to Graham Av.

❷ CHELSEA GARDEN OF EDEN $$ ♥
An incredible selection of high-quality products. Grocery, butcher, baker, dairy, fish market, fruits and vegetables, drinks, sushi, prepared meals, cocktail trays, gift baskets—all can be found in this immense store that looks like a European market.
162 W 23rd St., New York, NY 10011.
Subway: 1 to 23 St.

❸ UNION SQUARE MONDAY GREENMARKET $$
The most famous organic market in the city, closed Tuesdays, Thursdays, and Sundays. Up to 140 vendors and all sorts of products. Cooking demonstrations on certain days. Tables and chairs are available for tasting. A must!
E 17th St. and Union Square W, New York, NY 10003. Subway: N, Q, R, 4, 5, 6, L to 14 St.–Union Sq.

❹ WHOLE FOODS MARKET $$
The famous organic supermarket chain where you find absolutely everything! Also has quality prepared meals to eat on the spot or to take out.
4 Union Sq. S., New York, NY 10003.
Subway: N, Q, R, 4, 5, 6, L to 14 St.–Union Sq.

❺ WESTERLY NATURAL MARKET $$
Herb bar, soup bar, and lots of organic fruits and vegetables.
911 8th Ave., New York, NY 10019.
Subway: N, Q, R to 57 St.-7 Av.

❻ AGATA & VALENTINA $$$
Tasty Italian grocery store, with excellent products and sandwiches.
1505 1st Ave., New York, NY 10075.
Subway: 1 to 77 St.

❼ ZABAR'S $$
One of the oldest delicatessens in Manhattan, a true Aladdin's cave for gourmets. Breakfast to eat-in, meals to take-away. Many European specialties. A delight for the eyes and nose.
2245 Broadway, New York, NY 10024.
Subway: 1 to 79 St.

❽ TRADER JOE'S $
A beacon of the eco-organic trend. No online sales and few name-brand articles, but there's seasonal fruits and vegetables, stock that turns over quickly, and a variety of products.
2073 Broadway, New York, NY 10023.
Subway: 1, 2, 3 to 72 St.

❾ BEST MARKET $$
The best organic products in Harlem.
2187 Frederick Douglass Blvd., New York, NY 10026.
Subway: C, B to 116 St.

❿ SERENGETI TEAS & SPICES $$
Rigorous selection of teas from around the world.
2292 Frederick Douglass Blvd., New York, NY 10027.
Subway: A, C, B, D to 125 St.

⓫ SUN'S ORGANIC TEA SHOP $$ ♥
A friendly shop with a very complete selection of bulk loose teas.
79 Bayard St., New York, NY 10013.
Subway: J, Z to Canal St.

⓬ SMORGASBURG $$
One of the best local market products in Brooklyn, open in spring and summer. Over 100 stands, with cuisine from around the world: a delight!
Rotating locations: Check www.brooklynflea.com for details.

⓭ TINO'S DELICATESSEN $
A half-century-old deli in the Bronx.
2410 Arthur Ave., Bronx, NY 10458.
Subway: B, D to Fordham Road

⓮ ARTHUR AVENUE RETAIL MARKET $$
Adorable covered market in the heart of Little Italy in the Bronx.
2321 Hughes Ave., Bronx, NY 10458.
Subway: B, D to Fordham Road

⓯ KATAGIRI $$
The oldest Japanese grocery in the United States, which has been importing traditional products, edible or not, for over a century. Noodles, saké, spices, soya...Fresh seafood delivered daily.
224 E 59th St., New York, NY 10022.
Subway: 4, 5, 6 to 59 St.

MARIE ASSÉNAT

38 SWEET TREATS

Whether it's sunny or raining, there's always time for sweets. Sugar, chocolate, whipped cream, or buttercream, extravagance is not only reflected in the city's architecture: from Oreo-peanut-butter or red-velvet cupcakes to melt-in-your-mouth cookies and brownies, here are fifteen sweet stops that should satisfy every sweet tooth!

❶ MAGNOLIA BAKERY $$
Multicolored cupcakes favored by the heroines of *Sex and the City*.
200 Columbus Ave., New York, NY 10023. Subway: 1, 2, 3 to 72 St.

❷ CAFÉ SABARSKY $$
A Viennese café in the Neue Galerie–very chic, very cozy–offering traditional Austrian dishes and sweets. Try the delicious apple strudel and divine hot chocolate.
1048 5th Ave., New York, NY 10028. Subway: 4, 5, 6 to 86 St.

❸ LA BERGAMOTE $$
European-style tearoom in Chelsea. A superb choice: Pompadour (cake with Grand Marnier hazelnut mousse), Concorde (cake made with chocolate meringue, chocolate mousse and chocolate shavings…for chocolate addicts!).
177 9th Ave., New York, NY 10011. Subway: C, E to 23 St.

❹ ALMONDINE BAKERY $$
Bread, croissants, and pastries just like in Paris.
85 Water St., Brooklyn, NY 11201. Subway: F to York St.

❺ FINANCIER PATISSERIE $$
Eclairs and *pains au chocolat* galore. A financier, the little French cake with an almond base, is served with coffee.
62 Stone St., New York, NY 10004. Subway: J, Z to Broad St.

❻ MAX BRENNER $$
One of the best hot chocolates in town.
841 Broadway, New York, NY 10003. Subway: N, Q, R, 4, 5, 6, L to 14 St.–Union Sq.

❼ PASTICCERIA ROCCO $
Wonderful cannoli, perfectly fresh, and filled with cream while you wait.
243 Bleecker St., New York, NY 10014. Subway: A, C, E, B, D, F, M to W 4 St.

❽ CAFÉ ANGELIQUE $
A French pause in the heart of Greenwich Village.
68 Bleecker St., New York, NY 10012. Subway: 6 to Bleecker St.

❾ RICE TO RICHES $$
Astonishingly colorful and fragrant rice-based desserts.
37 Spring St., New York, NY 10012. Subway: 6 to Spring St.

❿ BILLY'S BAKERY $ ♥
Unmissable Manhattan pastry shop with a lovely decor. Hot chocolate with marshmallows to die for.
184 9th Ave., New York, NY 10011. Subway: C, E to 23 St.

⓫ LITTLE PIE COMPANY $$
Delicious tarts to recharge your batteries.
424 W 43rd St., New York, NY 10036. Subway: C, E to 50 St.

⓬ CAFÉ GRUMPY $
A pretty little place wafting with aromas (it's a café and a coffee roaster).
224 W 20th St., New York, NY 10011. Subway: 1 to 18 St.

⓭ IRVING FARM COFFEE ROASTERS $$
A typical New York café that, among other things, offers homemade baked goods!
71 Irving Pl., New York, NY 10003. Subway: 6 to 23 St.

⓮ LEVAIN BAKERY $$ ♥
The best cookies in Manhattan.
167 W 74th St., New York, NY 10023. Subway: 1, 2, 3 to 72 St.

⓯ MAKE MY CAKE $$
Extravagant cakes in bright colors.
121 St. Nicholas Ave., New York, NY 10026. Subway: C, B to 116 St.

ÉRIC GIRIAT

39 EXOTIC TASTES

The remarkable diversity of New York's population is wonderfully reflected in its gastronomic offerings. From tagine to pad thai by way of tacos, croques monsieur, or tapas, you can always find something to satisfy the most exotic cravings.

❶ BALTHAZAR $$$ ♥
Famous French brasserie with absolutely magnificent decor. The restaurant has its own bakery, so the bread and breakfasts are delicious.
80 Spring St., New York, NY 10012.
Subway: 6 to Spring St.

❷ KELLEY AND PING $$
Plentiful and authentic Chinese cuisine based on classics and inspired by street food. A wide selection of teas are served. Very pretty setting and friendly atmosphere.
127 Greene St., New York, NY 10012.
Subway: B, D, F, M to Broadway–Lafayette St.

❸ L'ÉCOLE $$$
Meals cooked by students of the French Culinary Institute. On the menu are traditional French dishes such as beef bourguignon and seared duck breast, and also an orange-flavored cake made with olive oil.
462 Broadway, New York, NY 10013.
Subway: 6 to Spring St.

❹ LOCANDA VERDE $$$
An Italian tavern serving tasty dishes in SoHo.
377 Greenwich St., New York, NY 10013.
Subway: 1 to Canal St.

❺ CAFÉ GITANE $$
French-Moroccan specialties in this hip restaurant with warm-toned colors. Red-leather banquettes, checkered napkins, French-style breakfasts and Moroccan-style couscous.
242 Mott St., New York, NY 10012.
Subway: 6 to Spring St.

❻ NOM WAH TEA PARLOR $$ ♥
Fried shrimp and steamed dumplings in an upscale diner atmosphere in central Chinatown.
13 Doyers St., New York, NY 10013.
Subway: J, Z to Canal St.

❼ PEASANT $$$
Famous Tuscan cuisine.
194 Elizabeth St., New York, NY 10012.
Subway: 6 to Spring St.

❽ LA ESQUINA $$
Organic Mexican cuisine. The tacos are fantastic.
114 Kenmare St., New York, NY 10012.
Subway: 6 to Spring St.

❾ SMÖRGÅS CHEF $$
Scandinavian cuisine is in the spotlight in an inviting setting.
53 Stone St., New York, NY 10004.
Subway: J, Z to Broad St.

❿ AMOR CUBANO $$
Famous Cuban cooking in the heart of East Harlem.
2018 3rd Ave., New York, NY 10029.
Subway: 6 to 110 St.

⓫ TROPICAL GRILL $
The best Dominican cuisine.
2145 Adam Clayton Powell Jr. Blvd., New York, NY 10027.
Subway: 2, 3 to 125 St.

⓬ MASSAWA $$
Ethiopian and Eritrean specialties.
1239 Amsterdam Ave., New York, NY 10027. Subway: 1 to 116 St.

⓭ BCD TOFU HOUSE $$ ♥
Excellent vegetarian Korean diner.
5 W 32nd St., New York, NY 10001.
Subway: N, Q, R, B, D, F, M to 34 St.–Herald Sq.

⓮ LA CAYE $$
Colorful and generous Creole cooking.
35 Lafayette Ave., New York, NY 11217.
Subway: A, C, J, Z, 2, 3, 4, 5 to Fulton St.

⓯ TAMARIND TRIBECA $$$ ♥
One of the best Indian restaurants in the city.
99 Hudson St., New York, NY 10013.
Subway: 1 to Franklin St.

BENEDITA FEIJÓ

40 EATS ON THE STREET

Street food is an international form of sustenance. Often inexpensive and delicious, in New York it's become an institution. Fast Halal, quick Kosher, hot dogs, sandwiches, and especially hamburgers with the works and you're satisfied in less than ten minutes. In New York everyone is in a hurry, and food trucks are everywhere, making it possible to eat on the run, phone glued to your ear, in the middle of a conference call or between appointments. An essential time-saver in a city where every minute counts.

1 ESSEX ST. MARKET $
A 1940s covered market full of enticing stands.
120 Essex St., New York, NY 10002. Subway: F, J, M, Z to Delancey St.

2 CALEXICO $
The best take-out burritos in Manhattan. Prince St. and Wooster St., New York, NY 10012. Subway: N, R to Prince St.

3 KORILLA BBQ $$
Korean-Mexican fusion, with yummy burritos, rice bowls, and salads. Several Manhattan locations. Follow the truck on Twitter: @KorillaBBQ

4 THE CINNAMON SNAIL $ ♥
Excellent vegan cuisine. Several Manhattan locations. Follow the truck on Twitter: @VeganLunchTruck

5 CORRADO BREAD AND PASTRY $ ♥
Delicious sandwiches between two museum visits.
960 Lexington Ave., New York, NY 10021. Subway: 6 to 68 St.– Hunter College

6 BIAN DANG TRUCK $
Authentic and generous Thai dishes. 53rd St. and Park Ave., New York, NY 10003. Subway: E, M to 5 Av-53 St.

7 WAFELS & DINGES $
All sorts of waffles sold from a bright yellow truck. Several Manhattan locations: Follow the truck on Twitter @waffletruck or Call HOT WAFELINE (866-429-7329)

8 NY DOSAS $ ♥
Said to be the best Indian fast food in New York.
50 Washington Sq. S., New York, NY 10014. Subway: A, C, E, B, D, F, M to W 4 St.

9 SOUVLAKI GR TRUCK $
A little taste of Greece in a sandwich. Several Manhattan locations. Follow the truck on Twitter: @souvlakitruck

10 FIVE GUYS BURGERS AND FRIES $
The Five Guys special? A burger and fries!
36 W 48th St., New York, NY 10036. Subway: B, D, F, M to 47-50 Sts.– Rockefeller Center

11 GROM $
The hippest gelato parlor of the moment. 233 Bleecker St., New York, NY 10014. Subway: A, C, E, B, D, F, M to W 4 St.

12 NATHAN'S FAMOUS $
Famous name hot dogs, opened since 1916.
1310 Surf Ave., Brooklyn, NY 11224. Subway: B, D, N, Q to Coney Island– Stillwell Av.

13 IL LABORATORIO DEL GELATO $ ♥
Ice-cream supplier of the city's best restaurants.
188 Ludlow St., New York, NY 10002. Subway: F to 2 Av.

14 MORRIS TRUCK $
Delicious grilled cheese sandwiches in the purest tradition. Several Manhattan locations. Follow the truck on Twitter: @morristruck

15 HALAL GUYS $ ♥
Best chicken and rice in town.
1330 6th Ave., New York, NY 10019. Subway: B, D, E to 7 Av.

41 FESTIVE NEW YORK

Whether it's Christmas carols, a mermaid parade, or an annual marathon, there is always something happening in New York. The city calendar is teeming with events, festivals, and parades, and the Cinco de Mayo, St. Patrick's Day, and the rainbow-decked Gay Pride parades remind us how the city's heart beats to the rhythm of the communities that compose it.

❶ TRIBECA FILM FESTIVAL ♥
The independent film festival, co-founded by Robert De Niro, takes place in spring (during the second half of April).
Various locations in the TriBeCa neighborhood depending on the year.

❷ GAY PRIDE
The parade, which is in support of gay rights, usually takes place the last Sunday of June. It's the most extravagant show of the year. W 36th St. and 5th Ave., New York, NY 10016. Subway: B, D, F, M, N, Q, R to 34th St.–Penn Station

❸ ST. PATRICK'S DAY
Irish Catholic feast day on March 17. Party all day and through the night; the city is very attached to this ritual, and the beer flows freely.
Parade Departure: 5th Ave. and 44th St., New York, NY 10036. Subway: 4, 5, 6, 7, S to Grand Central–42 St.

❹ CINCO DE MAYO ♥
Celebration of Mexico's victory against Napoleon III's troops in 1862.
Parade Departure: 33rd St. and 6th Ave., New York, NY 10001. Subway: N, Q, R, B, D, F, M to 34 St.–Herald Sq.

❺ LUNAR NEW YEAR CELEBRATION AND FESTIVAL
Fireworks and parades to celebrate the Chinese New Year, in January or February. Chinatown, around Canal St., New York, NY 10013.
Subway: J, N, Q, R, Z, 6 to Canal St.

❻ NEW YORK FILM FESTIVAL
For over 40 years this festival has been organized in September by the Film Society of Lincoln Center. 70 Lincoln Center Plaza, New York, NY 10023. Subway: 1 to 66 St.–Lincoln Center

❼ VILLAGE HALLOWEEN PARADE ♥
Extravagant costume parade through the streets of the Village.
Parade Departure: 6th Ave. and Canal St., New York, NY 10013. Subway: C, E to Spring St.

❽ FREE SHAKESPEARE IN THE PARK (AT DELACORTE THEATER)
Free outdoor performances of Shakespeare plays (summer only). 81 Central Park West, New York, NY 10023. Subway: C, B to 81 St.–Museum of Natural History

❾ INDEPENDENCE DAY
Fourth of July fireworks on the Hudson River.
Best view: Brooklyn Heights Promenade, from Orange St. to Joralemon St., along the East River, Brooklyn, NY 11201. Subway: 2, 3 to Clark St.

❿ MOSTLY MOZART FESTIVAL
Free classical music concerts at Lincoln Center in summer. 10 Lincoln Center Plaza, New York, NY 10023. Subway: 1 to 66 St.–Lincoln Center

⓫ COLUMBUS DAY
A parade celebrating the discovery of America by Christopher Columbus; held the second Monday of October.
Parade Departure: 5th Ave. and 44th St., New York, NY 10036. Subway: 4, 5, 6, 7, S to Grand Central–42 St.

⓬ MACY'S THANKSGIVING DAY PARADE
The biggest parade of the year.
Parade Departure: W 77th St. and Central Park West, New York, NY 10024. Subway: C, B to 81 St.–Museum of Natural History

⓭ THREE KINGS DAY PARADE
Parade of children, donkeys, and sheep in East Harlem on the eve of the Epiphany.
Parade Departure: E 106th St. and Lexington Ave., New York, NY 10029. Subway: 6 to 110 St.

⓮ MERMAID PARADE
The most eccentric of parades of mermaids in an erotic burlesque atmosphere, with floats, bizarre cars, and all sort of carriages; held the last Saturday of June.
Parade Departure: W 21st St. and Surf Ave., Brooklyn, NY 11224. Subway: B, D, N, Q to Coney Island–Stillwell Av.

⓯ TCS NEW YORK CITY MARATHON
One of the world's most famous marathons takes place the first Sunday of November. You must register between January and February. Each country has a quota of participants, who are chosen by lottery.
Departure from Staten Island, finish line in Central Park (by way of Brooklyn and Queens).

QUENTIN VIJOUX

42 MANHATTAN COCKTAILS

It is no surprise that the Manhattan, a cocktail consisting of whiskey, vermouth, and a dash of bitters invented in the 1870s, is now famous around the world. Bars have always been the backbone of New York social life, whether for meeting up with old friends or making new ones.

1 ROSE BAR (IN GRAMERCY PARK HOTEL) $$$ ♥
Excellent cocktails and cozy and romantic ambiance (by candlelight). A stylish place where you can admire the works of Jean-Michel Basquiat or Keith Haring. The HQ of actors, top models, and singers.
2 Lexington Ave., New York, NY 10010.
Subway: 6 to 23 St.

2 THE STANDARD BIERGARTEN (AT STANDARD HIGH LINE HOTEL) $$
At the foot of the High Line: beer, sausages, and Ping-Pong tables. No garden despite the name, but a very friendly atmosphere. A waiting queue every night!
848 Washington St., New York, NY 10014. Subway: A, C, E, L to 8 Av.

3 BLUE BAR (IN THE ALGONQUIN HOTEL TIMES SQ.) $$$$
A preferred meeting place for the city's intellectuals. Chic and subdued ambiance, impeccable staff, good but pricey cocktails.
59 W 44th St., New York, NY 10036.
Subway: 1, 2, 3, S, A, C, E, N, Q, R, 7 to Times Square–42 St.

4 230 FIFTH $$$
A spectacular view (one of the finest of the Empire State Building) from a rooftop terrace planted with palm trees. Partially heated in the cooler months.
230 5th Ave., New York, NY 10001.
Subway: 6 to 28 St.

5 SALON DE NING (THE PENINSULA HOTEL) $$$$
A snug 1930s Shanghai atmosphere.
700 5th Ave., New York, NY 10019.
Subway: E, M to 5 Av–53 St.

6 FLATIRON LOUNGE $$$
An art deco cocktail bar.
37 W 19th St., New York, NY 10011.
Subway: N, R to 23 St.

7 FEATHERWEIGHT $$ ♥
Perfect service, original cocktails—one of the best bars in town.
135 Graham Ave., Brooklyn, NY 11206.
Subway: L to Montrose Av.

8 MCSORLEY'S OLD ALE HOUSE $
One of New York's oldest Irish pubs, an atmosphere full of character.
15 E 7th St., New York, NY 10003.
Subway: 6 to Astor Pl.

9 PULSE KARAOKE LOUNGE & SUITES $$
For singing till the end of the night.
135 W 41st St., New York, NY 10036.
Subway: 1, 2, 3, S, A, C, E, N, Q, R, 7 to Times Square–42 St.

10 SWIFT HIBERNIAN LOUNGE $$
The authenticity and warmth of a traditional pub.
34 E 4th St., New York, NY 10003.
Subway: 6 to Astor Pl.

11 THE PRESS LOUNGE $$$ ♥
An unrestricted view over midtown and the Hudson.
653 11th Ave., 16th Fl., New York, NY 10036. Subway: C, E to 50 St.

12 PLEASE DON'T TELL (IN CRIF DOGS) $$$
A famous speakeasy hidden inside a gourmet hot dog restaurant.
113 St. Marks Pl., New York, NY 10009.
Subway: L to 1 Av.

13 NUYORICAN POETS CAFE $
A bohemian underground institution since the 1970s.
236 E 3rd St., New York, NY 10009.
Subway: F, J, M, Z to Essex St.

14 THE GINGER MAN $$
A fantastic selection of local and imported beers.
11 E 36th St., New York, NY 10016.
Subway: 6 to 33 St.

15 ANGEL'S SHARE (IN VILLAGE YOKOCHO) $$$
Cocktail bar hidden upstairs in a Japanese restaurant.
8 Stuyvesant St., New York, NY 10003.
Subway: 6 to Astor Pl.

MORNING SIDE HEIGHTS HAMILTON HEIGHTS MARCUS GARVEY PARK

HARLEM APOLLO THEATRE, ABYSSINIAN BAPTIST CHURCH, STUDIO MUSEUM IN HARLEM, SUGAR HILL, STRIVER'S ROW

UPPER WEST SIDE MERICAN USEUM OF NATURAL HISTORY, 'ENTRAL PARK COLUMBUS CIRCLE

UPPER EAST SIDE FRICK COLLECTION, CENTRAL PARK, THE MET, WHITNEY MUSEUM OF AMERICAN ART, GUGGENHEIM MUSEUM

MIDTOWN MoMA, BRYANT PARK TOP OF THE ROCK, NYPL

GRAMERCY EMPIRE STATE BUILDING, GRAND CENTRL TERMINAL, CHRYSLER BUILDING

REENWICH VILLAGE LEECKER STREET, IE ROW, SHINGTON UARE PARK

EAST VILLAGE ST. MARKS PLACE, TOMPKINS SQUARE PARK, THE HOLE

SOHO DRAWING CENTRE, NEWYORK CITY FIRE MUSEUM

LOWER EAST SIDE NEW MUSEUM, ESSEX STREET MARKET,

ORCHARD STREET

CHINATOWN COLUMBUS PARK, KIMLAU SQUARE MOCA

FINANCIAL DISTRICT BROOKLYN BRIDGE, GOVERNORS ISLAND, BATTERY PARK

BOWLING GREEN, CITY HALL

HYESU LEE

43 LIVE IN NEW YORK

From prestigious Manhattan concert halls to underground scenes in Brooklyn, whether you are a classical music lover; punk enthusiast; folk, rock, or country fan, you're sure to find a venue that fits your style. So relax, have a drink, let the night pass by and simply enjoy the music you love.

① RADIO CITY MUSIC HALL ♥
A magnificent art deco auditorium. The shimmering stage curtain is the largest in the world.
1260 6th Ave., New York, NY 10020.
Subway: B, D, F, M to 47–50 Sts.–Rockefeller Center

② CARNEGIE HALL
Classical, pop, jazz, or contemporary music orchestras. This auditorium, inaugurated in 1891, was where the New York Philharmonic played between 1892 and 1962.
881 7th Ave., New York, NY 10019.
Subway: N, Q, R to 57 St.–7 Av.

③ METROPOLITAN OPERA
Marvel at a ballet or an opera in this magnificent auditorium simply known as the "Met" and located in Lincoln Center, home to twelve major New York performing arts companies.
30 Lincoln Center Plaza, New York, NY 10023. Subway: 1 to 66 St.–Lincoln Center

④ ARLENE'S GROCERY $$
Monday evening rock concerts and punk karaoke.
95 Stanton St., New York, NY 10002.
Subway: F to 2 Av.

⑤ ROCKWOOD MUSIC HALL $$
Three small bars and three small concert stages to discover talented groups. Quality folk-rock music.
196 Allen St., New York, NY 10002.
Subway: F to 2 Av.

⑥ MERCURY LOUNGE $$
A renowned, independent rock scene. This small but very comfortable lounge will appeal to fans of alternative rock.
217 E Houston St., New York, NY 10002.
Subway: F to 2 Av.

⑦ SILVANA $$
African-Israeli basement club with demanding and invigorating programming.
300 W 116th St., New York, NY 10026.
Subway: C, B to 116 St.

⑧ BARGEMUSIC $$
Chamber music concerts in a lovely intimate setting.
2 Old Fulton St., Brooklyn, NY 11201.
Subway: F to York St.

⑨ BAM/PETER JAY SHARP BUILDING
Numerous concerts in the oldest US arts center; founded in 1861.
30 Lafayette Ave., Brooklyn, NY 11217.
Subway: Fulton St.

⑩ PETE'S CANDY STORE $ ♥
Quizzes, games, and intimate concerts in the little room at the back. Party ambiance until the wee hours in this former candy store. A must-see destination in Brooklyn.
709 Lorimer St., Brooklyn, NY 11211.
Subway: L to Lorimer St.

⑪ MUSIC HALL OF WILLIAMSBURG $$ ♥
The famous Williamsburg music venue.
66 N 6th St., Brooklyn, NY 11211.
Subway: L to Bedford Av.

⑫ CAFFÈ VIVALDI $$
A place for lovers of music and good, healthy, quality cuisine. Featuring jazz and classical music programming.
32 Jones St, New York, NY 10014.
Subway: A, C, E, B, D, F, M to W 4 St.

⑬ THE BOWERY BALLROOM
A historic rock concert hall on the Lower East Side.
6 Delancey St., New York, NY 10002.
Subway: J, Z to Bowery

⑭ BEACON THEATER
A magnificent theater where the hippie generation came to listen to the Allman Brothers' final show.
2124 Broadway, New York, NY 10023.
Subway: 1, 2, 3 to 72 St.

⑮ THE TOWN HALL
Where you'll hear some of the best acoustics in town.
123 W 43rd St., New York, NY 10036.
Subway: 1, 2, 3, A, C, E, N, Q, R, 7, S to Times Square.–42 St.

JACOPO ROSATI

44 JAZZY NEW YORK

Throughout the twentieth century, New York was one of the major jazz scenes, from the genre's birth to its worldwide influence. Today, many legendary clubs continue to open their doors to an audience of fans looking for the next Miles Davis or Charlie Parker.

❶ BLUE NOTE $$$
Listen to excellent music while sipping a cocktail in this legendary club. The list of artists who have performed in this jazz temple is long: Ray Charles, John Coltrane, Dizzy Gillespie, Keith Jarrett, Oscar Peterson...
131 W 3rd St., New York, NY 10012.
Subway: A, C, E, B, D, F, M to W 4 St.

❷ IRIDIUM $$$
A leading midtown venue for mesmerizing jazz sessions. This club has introduced iconic guitarists like Les Paul, Jeff Beck, and Zakk Wylde.
1650 Broadway, New York, NY 10019.
Subway: N, Q, R to 49 St.

❸ VILLAGE VANGUARD $$
Savor every note in this basement club where John Coltrane, Miles Davis, and Bill Evans have played. Pure jazz atmosphere in a contemplative silence: no photos, no recordings, no telephones, no eating, no small talk...
178 7th Ave. S, New York, NY 10014.
Subway: 1, 2, 3 to 14 St.

❹ APOLLO THEATER $$
A legendary scene that hosted the first performances of American black music.
253 W 125th St., New York, NY 10027.
Subway: A, C, B, D to 125 St.

❺ BIRDLAND $$$
"The jazz corner of the world," as the sign says.
315 W 44th St., New York, NY 10036.
Subway: N, Q, R to 49 St.

❻ DIZZY'S CLUB COCA-COLA $$$
Enjoy a jazz tune while taking in the view of Central Park.
10 Columbus Circle, New York, NY 10019. Subway: A, C, B, D, 1 to 59th St.-Columbus Circle

❼ PARIS BLUES $$ ♥
A Harlem institution since 1969, offering quality jazz evenings.
2021 Adam Clayton Powell Jr. Blvd., New York, NY 10027. Subway: 2, 3 to 125 St.

❽ THE STONE $
For jazz purists and the avant-garde.
E 2nd St. and Ave. C, New York, NY 10009. Subway: F, J, M, Z to Essex St.

❾ JAZZ STANDARD $$$
Great jazz scene and delicious barbecue specialties.
116 E 27th St., New York, NY 10016.
Subway: 6 to 28 St.

❿ SMOKE JAZZ & SUPPER CLUB $$$
One of the most renowned clubs on the West Side.
2751 Broadway, New York, NY 10025.
Subway: 1 to 103 St.

⓫ SHOWMAN'S $$
Old jazz in this long and narrow, friendly room.
375 W 125th St., New York, NY 10027.
Subway: A, C, B, D to 125 St.

⓬ MINTON'S $$$$ ♥
Formerly Minton's Playhouse and opened in 1938 by the famous saxophonist Henry Minton.
206 W 118th St., New York, NY 10026.
Subway: B, C to 116 St.

⓭ BILL'S PLACE $
A Harlem brownstone turned B.Y.O.B. jazz club on Friday and Saturday nights. Renowned saxophonist and owner Bill Saxton plays here.
148 W 133rd St., New York, NY 10030.
Subway: 2, 3 to 135 St.

⓮ COTTON CLUB $$ ♥
The recently reopened famous Harlem jazz club.
656 W 125th St., New York, NY 10027.
Subway: 1 to 125 St.

⓯ SMALLS JAZZ CLUB
As tiny as it is authentic. It's an unmissable place for discovering new talent.
183 W 10th St., New York, NY 10014.
Subway: 1 to Christopher St.-Sheridan Square

MIGUEL PORLAN

45 HIP-HOP HISTORY

New York is the birthplace of hip-hop, the music genre that grew from the streets of all five boroughs. It's here that some of the greatest American rappers emerged, including the Notorious B.I.G., Jay Z, and Mos Def. Discover the roots of this culture, once subversive, now known worldwide.

❶ NEW ERA $$$
Large selection of baseball caps favored by rappers.
9 E 4th St., New York, NY 10003.
Subway: 6 to Astor Pl.

❷ ALIFE $$$
The temple of streetwear.
158 Rivington St., New York, NY 10002.
Subway: F, J, M, Z to Essex St.

❸ DJ KOOL HERC'S HOUSE
The building of the founding father of hip-hop, where the first block parties happened.
1520 Sedgwick Ave., Bronx, NY 10453.
Subway: 4 to 176 St.

❹ WEINSTEIN HALL (AT NYU)
Rick Rubin and Russell Simmons founded the precursor of the hip-hop label Def Jam Recordings in this universtiy dormitory.
University Pl., New York, NY 10003.
Subway: N, R to 8 St.–NYU

❺ THE FREESTYLE OF THE NOTORIOUS B.I.G.
It was on this corner that the flow of the artist dubbed "Biggie," mesmerized crowds for the first time.
Bedford Ave. and Quincy St., Brooklyn, NY 11221. Subway: G to Bedford-Nostrand Avs.

❻ DR JAY'S $$ ♥
A top destination for urban fashion.
33 W 34 th St., New York, NY 10001.
Subway: N, Q, R, B, D, F, M to 34 St.–Herald Sq.

❼ BIG L'S CORNER $$ ♥
Sad corner of this Harlem neighborhood, where the rapper Big L was murdered in front of his home, on February 15, 1999, at the age of 24.
45 W 139th St., New York, NY 10037.
Subway: 2, 3 to 135 St.

❽ SOB'S $$ ♥
SOB's (Sound of Brazil) is a salsa club transformed into a prestigious hip-hop concert hall. You can also have brunch, lunch, dinner, or just a drink.
204 Varick St., New York, NY 10014.
Subway: 1 to Houston St.

❾ 226 SAINT JAMES PL.
The rapper Notorious B.I.G. grew up on the third floor of this building. He was murdered on March 9, 1997, at the age of 24.
226 St. James Pl., Brooklyn, NY 11238.
Subway: C to Clinton–Washington Avs.

❿ FORT GREENE
Birthplace of 1990s progressive hip-hop, as found in the music of Gang Starr and Mos Def.
Around Fort Greene Park, Myrtle Ave., Brooklyn, NY 11201. Subway: B, R to Fulton St.

⓫ HIGH ST. STATION
In the video for their song "Root Down," legendary hip-hop group Beastie Boys climbed on the train at this station.
High St. Station, Brooklyn, NY 11201.
Subway: A, C to High St.

⓬ FULTON STREET MALL
Pedestrian street lined with over one hundred stores to buy an essential hip-hop wardrobe.
356 Fulton St., Brooklyn, NY 11201.
Subway: 2, 3 to Hoyt St.

⓭ 560 STATE STREET
A building where dozens of hip-hop artists lived in the 1990s, including rapper Jay Z.
560 State St., Brooklyn, NY 11217.
Subway: B, Q, 2, 3, 4, 5 to Atlantic Av.–Barclays Center

⓮ SUGAR HILL
Harlem neighborhood of the Sugarhill Gang, whose song "Rapper's Delight" is said to have popularized rap music.
Between W. 155th St., 145th St., Edgecombe Ave. and Amsterdam Ave
Subway: C to 155 St.

⓯ MUSIC MATTERS
Excellent collection of old-school hip-hop.
413 7th Ave., Brooklyn, NY 11215.
Subway: F, G to 7 Av.

SARAH A. KING

46 ON BROADWAY

Just off Times Square, the neon lights and giant screens of Broadway theaters continue to keep the American music-hall legend alive. *Mamma Mia!, Hair,* and *Phantom of the Opera*: the mythical titles shine side-by-side on the glittering marquees of the entertainment capital of the world!

1 STUDIO 54
After having been a discotheque, theater, and CBS televsion studio, Studio 54 is now home to the Roundabout Theater Company.
254 W 54th St., New York, NY 10019.
Subway: N, Q, R to 57 St.-7 Av.

2 AUGUST WILSON THEATER
Opened in 1925, this Broadway theater often changed its name, and finally took that of playwright August Wilson in 2005.
245 W 52nd St., New York, NY 10019.
Subway: B, D, E to 7 Av.

3 BROADWAY THEATER
Former cinema famous for having hosted numerous film premieres, this vast auditorium regularly stages musicals.
1681 Broadway, New York, NY 10019.
Subway: B, D, E to 7 Av.

4 NEIL SIMON THEATER
The former Alvin Theater was inaugurated in 1927 with *Funny Face*, a Gershwin musical featuring Fred Astaire.
250 W 52nd St., New York, NY 10019.
Subway: C, E to 50 St.

5 GERSHWIN THEATER
The auditorium having the largest capacity on Broadway, with over 1,900 seats.
222 W 51st St., New York, NY 10019.
Subway: C, E to 50 St.

6 BARRYMORE THEATER
A Streetcar Named Desire, by Tennessee Williams, played here.
243 W 47th St., New York, NY 10036.
Subway: N, Q, R to 49 St.

7 THE ACTORS STUDIO
Elia Kazan cofounded it in 1947, and Lee Strasberg taught the greatest here: Marlon Brando, Al Pacino, Marilyn Monroe...
432 W 44th St., New York, NY 10036.
Subway: A, C, E, 1, 2, 3, S, L, N, Q, R, 7 to 42 St.-Port Authority Bus Terminal

8 NEW AMSTERDAM THEATER ♥
The theater has been magnificently restored to its original Art Deco style.
214 W 42nd St., New York, NY 10036.
Subway: A, C, E, 1, 2, 3, N, Q, R, S, 7 to Times Sq.

9 LUNT-FONTANNE THEATER
Prior to paying tribute to the actors Alfred Lunt and Lynn Fontanne, this Broadway theater was called the Globe, the name of Shakespeare's theater in England.
205 W 46th St., New York, NY 10036.
Subway: N, Q, R to 49 St.

10 BROOKS ATKINSON THEATER
It was named after the famous *New York Times* theater critic.
256 W 47th St., New York, NY 10036.
Subway: N, Q, R to 49 St.

11 PALACE THEATER
Its stage has featured Judy Garland, Jerry Lewis, Harry Belafonte, Bette Midler, Shirley MacLaine, Diana Ross...
1564 Broadway, New York, NY 10036.
Subway: N, Q, R to 49 St.

12 IMPERIAL THEATER
Like many other Broadway theaters, such as Brooks Atkinson and the Majestic, it was designed by the architect Herbert J. Krapp.
249 W 45th St., New York, NY 10036.
Subway: N, Q, R to 49 St.

13 LYCEUM THEATER ♥
Built in the Beaux-Arts style, this theater is one of the oldest on Broadway, dating back to 1903.
149 W 45th St., New York, NY 10036.
Subway: N, Q, R to 49 St.

14 MARQUIS THEATER
Opened in 1986, this is one of the newer Broadway theaters.
1535 Broadway, New York, NY 10036.
Subway: N, Q, R to 49 St.

15 MAJESTIC THEATER ♥
Inaugurated in 1927, it has staged many famous productions, including *Porgy and Bess* and *Breakfast at Tiffany's*.
245 W 44th St., New York, NY 10036.
Subway: 1, 2, 3, S, 7, N, Q, R, A, C, E to 42 St.-Port Authority Bus Terminal

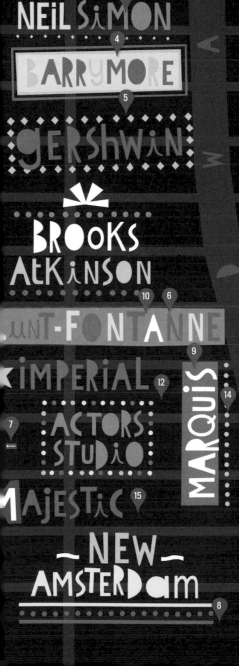

STUDIO 54

AUGUST WILSON

BROADWAY

1

3

NEIL SIMON

2

BARRYMORE

4

5

GERSHWIN

BROOKS ATKINSON

PALACE

10 6

...unT-FONTANNE

11

9

IMPERIAL

12

MARQUIS

LYCEUM

14

7

ACTORS STUDIO

13

MAJESTIC

15

~NEW~ AMSTERDAM

8

SOPHIE LEDESMA

47 GAME ON

Who said that games are just for kids? No one in New York, at any rate! The city abounds with establishments offering a countless number of games: billards, Foosball, pinball, darts, bowling, table tennis...

❶ BOWLMOR TIMES SQ. $$
Bowling lanes with wacky decor, inspired by the city's iconic places, such as Chinatown, Central Park, or Coney Island, for a very original atmosphere.
222 W 44th St., New York, NY 10036.
Subway: N, Q, R to 49 St.

❷ SLATE $$ ♥
Some dozen pool tables, along with Ping-Pong and Foosball.
54 W 21st St., New York, NY 10010.
Subway: F, M to 23 St.

❸ EASTSIDE BILLIARDS $$
One of the city's largest billiards halls. Sixteen pool tables, seven giant screens, and a cocktail bar.
163 E 86th St., New York, NY 10028.
Subway: 4, 5, 6 to 86 St.

❹ BROOKLYN BOWL $$
A bowling alley housed in a former factory.
61 Wythe Ave., Brooklyn, NY 11249.
Subway: G to Nassau Av.

❺ MONA'S $
This inexpensive, friendly bar is ideal for a game of pool in the East Village. There's jazz every Tuesday evening.
224 Ave. B, New York, NY 10009.
Subway: L to 1 Av.

❻ BARCADE $$ ♥
Large beer selection and arcade games, including the best 1980s and 1990s classics.
388 Union Ave., Brooklyn, NY 11211.
Subway: L to Metropolitan Av.

❼ KETTLE OF FISH $
Friendly, unpretentious bar, with pinball, darts, jukebox, and board games.
59 Christopher St., New York, NY 10014.
Subway: 1 to Christopher St.–Sheridan Sq.

❽ ACE BAR $
Excellent East Village bar, with pool, darts, and pinball.
531 E 5th St., New York, NY 10009.
Subway: F to 2 Av.

❾ AMSTERDAM BILLIARDS $$
A bar devoted to all kinds of games: pool, Foosball, darts...
110 E 11th St., New York, NY 10003.
Subway: 6 to Astor Pl.

❿ WICKED WILLY'S $
Here they play beer pong with a mix of skill and drunkenness.
149 Bleecker St., New York, NY 10012.
Subway: A, C, E, B, D, F, M to W 4 St.

⓫ MODERN PINBALL $
A pinball lover's paradise with 30 machines, from classics to new releases.
362 3rd Ave (at 26th St.), New York, NY 10016. Subway: 4, 6 to 28 St.

⓬ MINI GOLF (AT PIER 25)
To relax: mini golf course, surrounded by greenery, with wonderful views of the Statue of Liberty.
225 West St., New York, NY 10013.
Subway: 1 to Franklin St.

⓭ BROOKLYN GOLF CENTER
Eighteen-hole course, driving range, mini golf, and bucolic setting.
3200 Flatbush Ave., Brooklyn, NY 11234.
Subway: F to Av. U

⓮ UNION HALL $$
Bocce in a comfortable atmosphere, with sofas and fireplace.
702 Union St., Brooklyn, NY 11215.
Subway: 4, 5, 6, N, Q, R, L to 14th St–Union St.

⓯ FAT CAT $ ♥
Authentic bar, billiards, Ping-Pong, board games, and jazz concerts.
75 Christopher St., New York, NY 10014.
Subway: A, C, E, B, D, F, M to W 4 St.

TILT
00:12:10

PLAY TIME

MAXIME GARCIA

48 THE CITY THAT NEVER SLEEPS

The time on the clock means nothing in New York: you can have dinner at noon and breakfast at midnight, and neon lights replace the sun at dusk. It's a paradise for insomniacs and night owls! Whether you're looking for a snack, a drink, or need to fight the effects of jet lag, you will always find an open door in this city that never sleeps.

❶ CIELO $$$
Electro music in the Meatpacking district.
18 Little W 12th St., New York, NY 10014.
Subway: A, C, E, L to 14 St.

❷ WEBSTER HALL $$
Famous club, the largest in New York, with over four floors; right in the middle of the East Village.
125 E 11th St., New York, NY 10003.
Subway: L to 3 Av.

❸ KNITTING FACTORY $
The legendary club, formerly on Houston St., now in Williamsburg.
361 Metropolitan Ave., Brooklyn, NY 11211. Subway: L to Metropolitan Av.

❹ LANDMARK'S SUNSHINE CINEMA
Midnight show on Fridays and Saturdays, screening of classics and horror films.
143 E Houston St., New York, NY 10002.
Subway: F to 2 Av.

❺ THE BITTER END $$
Legendary Greenwich Village bar frequented by Stevie Wonder, Bob Dylan, Woody Allen, and many other greats (open until four a.m.).
147 Bleecker St., New York, NY 10012.
Subway: N, R to 8 St.–NYU

❻ WHITE HORSE TAVERN $$
Beers, good whiskey, a nineteenth-century bar that became a Greenwich Village bohemian hangout in the 1950s and '60s.
567 Hudson St., New York, NY 10014.
Subway: 1 to Christopher St.–Sheridan Sq.

❼ GREAT NY NOODLETOWN $
Delicious Chinese food, served until four a.m.
28 Bowery, New York, NY 10013.
Subway: J, Z to Canal St.

❽ DAISY'S DINER $ ♥
Breakfast—pancakes, bacon, and maple syrup—24/7.
452 5th Ave., Brooklyn, NY 11215.
Subway: F, G, R to 9 St.

❾ KELLOGG'S DINER $$ ♥
The meeting place of Brooklyn's insomniacs. More for the atmosphere than the food. Open 24/7.
518 Metropolitan Ave., Brooklyn, NY 11211. Subway: L to Lorimer St.

❿ MILANO'S BAR $
Slightly worn joint, inexpensive beer, and lively atmosphere until four a.m.
51 E Houston St., New York, NY 10012.
Subway: B, D, F, M to Broadway-Lafayette St.

⓫ LE BATEAU IVRE $$$
French bistro, good wine, open until four a.m.
230 E 51st St., New York, NY 10022.
Subway: E, M to Lexington Av.–53 St.

⓬ RYAN'S DAUGHTER $$
Classic Irish pub: beers on tap, unmissable pool tables, and dart games.
350 E 85th St., New York, NY 10028.
Subway: 4, 5, 6 to 86 St.

⓭ MISSION DOLORES $$
In a former garage; pinball, good beers, and veranda walls lined with photos of outlaws.
249 4th Ave., Brooklyn, NY 11215.
Subway: Union St.

⓮ UNION HALL $$
Play bocce on two lanes in a cozy setting.
702 Union St., Brooklyn, NY 11215.
Subway: Union St.

⓯ SUNNY'S BAR $
Century-old bar; friendly and inexpensive.
253 Conover St., Brooklyn, NY 11231.
Subway: F, G to Carroll St.

MARION ALFANO

49 SLEEPER HITS

Are you going to break the bank and offer yourself an unforgettable night at the Plaza? Or maybe attempt an urban camping experience in a tent perched on the roof of a Brooklyn building? With over 300 hotels in the city—from five-star to youth hostels—and a handful of atypical options, in the end, the hardest thing will be choosing which one.

1 THE MERCER $$$
One of the best hotels in SoHo. Discreet and ultra-cozy ambiance.
147 Mercer St., New York, NY 10012.
Subway: N, R to Prince St.

2 THE NOMAD HOTEL $$
Parisian atmosphere in the rooms of this immense building in Manhattan's NoMad neighborhood located between the Flatiron district and Korea Town.
1170 Broadway, New York, NY 10001.
Subway: N, R to 28 St.

3 SUGAR HILL HARLEM INN
Spacious, well-equipped rooms in this pleasant, unpretentious hotel.
460 W 141st St., New York, NY 10031.
Subway: 1 to 137 St.–City College

4 THE STANDARD HIGH LINE $$
Huge glass box: the view is breathtaking from the rooms.
848 Washington St., New York, NY 10014. Subway: A, C, E, L to 8 Av.

5 THE PIERRE $$ ♥
A legendary 1930s luxury hotel in granite and brick. The auras of Audrey Hepburn and Yves Saint Laurent still float through the air.
2 E 61st St., New York, NY 10065.
Subway: N, Q, R to 5 Av.–59 St.

6 LIBRARY HOTEL $$
The ten floors of this hotel have been organized according to the Dewey Decimal System, which classifies books according to subject matter. Guests have 6,000 books at their disposal.
299 Madison Ave., New York, NY 10017.
Subway: 4, 5, 6, 7 to Grand Central–42 St.

7 BIVOUAC NEW YORK
Camp in one of six tents set up on a rooftop? It's an idea of the artist Thomas Stevenson. Come with your sleeping bag and food to share. No electronics, no shower.
Locations change: Check with the site bivouacny.com

8 WYTHE HOTEL $$ ♥
Completely renovated industrial building from the early twentieth century. View of the skyline from the rooftop bar.
80 Wythe Ave., Brooklyn, NY 11249.
Subway: G to Nassau Av.

9 THE GREENWICH HOTEL $$$$
Charming. It's like being at home but with the added luxury of a spa and pool. Owned by Robert De Niro, in the TriBeCa neighborhood.
377 Greenwich St., New York, NY 10013.
Subway: 1 to Franklin St.

10 THE FRENCH QUARTERS GUEST APARTMENTS $$$
Furnished apartments, with breakfast included, and ideal for families.
346 W 46th St., New York, NY 10036.
Subway: C, E to 50 St.

11 THE HARLEM FLOPHOUSE $ ♥
Inexpensive rooms full of charm: parquet flooring and exposed beams.
242 W 123rd St., New York, NY 10027.
Subway: 2, 3 to 125 St.

12 THE JANE $$
Built in 1908, this West Village landmark was originally built as lodging for sailors, and has still retained its nautical charm.
113 Jane St., New York, NY 10014.
Subway: L to 8 Av.

13 THE HIGH LINE HOTEL $$
Located in the imposing Neo-Gothic buildings of an old nineteenth-century seminary; has a gorgeous garden.
180 10th Ave., New York, NY 10011.
Subway: C, E to 23 St.

14 HOTEL GIRAFFE $$$
Lovely establishment in central Manhattan. A very pleasant rooftop patio.
365 Park Ave. S, New York, NY 10016.
Subway: 6 to 28 St.

15 THE PLAZA HOTEL $$$$ ♥
Once said to be the most beautiful luxury hotel in the world. Immortalized in *The Great Gatsby* and *North by Northwest*. Starting price–650 dollars a night.
768 5th Ave., New York, NY 10019.
Subway: N, Q, R to 5 Av.–59 St.

THOMAS BURNS

50 BEYOND MANHATTAN

**Forget Midtown, the Empire State Building, and the streets of
Manhattan. Today the on-trend tourist travels to the outer boroughs.
Long overlooked, the Bronx, Queens, Brooklyn, and Staten Island–
driven by a new generation of artists and idealists–have finally woken
up, triggering a cultural wave that continues to transform New York.**

❶ COTTON CANDY MACHINE $$ ♥
Crazy shop and art gallery in a former
industrial building. Prints, posters,
clothing, books, toys created by
contemporary artists.
235 S 1st St., Brooklyn, NY 11211.
Subway: J, M, Z to Marcy Av.

❷ 718 CYCLERY $$
The stylish cyclist's New York temple.
Rent a bike and take off to explore
Brooklyn !
254 3rd Ave., Brooklyn, NY 11215.
Subway: R to Union St.

❸ MCCARREN PARK
The meeting spot of cool Brooklyn youth.
Lorimer St. and Manhattan Ave.,
between Bayard St. and Berry St.–
Nassau St., Brooklyn, NY 11222.
Subway: G to Nassau Av.

❹ FETTE SAU $$ ♥
Minimalist decor, industrial style, and
delicious grilled meats.
354 Metropolitan Ave., Brooklyn,
NY 11211. Subway: L to Bedford Av.

❺ BUSHWICK COUNTRY CLUB $ ♥
Typical of Brooklyn: an old photo booth, a
dilapidated mini golf, and cheap drinks.
618 Grand St., Brooklyn, NY 11211.
Subway: L to Metropolitan Av.

❻ BROOKLYN BOTANIC GARDEN
Tropical plants and Japanese temples.
1000 Washington Ave., Brooklyn,
NY 11225. Subway: 2, 3, 4, 5, S to
Botanic Garden

❼ CYCLONE (IN LUNA PARK) $$
Wooden roller coaster dating from 1927,
one of the most famous rides in America.
1000 Surf Ave., Brooklyn, NY 11224.
Subway: F, Q to W 8 St.–NY Aquarium

**❽ JANE'S CAROUSEL
(BROOKLYN BRIDGE PARK) $**
A children's merry-go-round, also
enjoyed by adults. Has a lovely view.
Dock St., Brooklyn, NY 11201.
Subway: R to Court St.

❾ KINGS COUNTY DISTILLERY $$
New York's oldest operating whiskey
distillery.
299 Sands St. Bldg 121, Brooklyn,
NY 11205. Subway: A, C to High St.

❿ MOMA PS1
Contemporary arts center founded in
1971 by Alanna Heiss and affiliated with
the MoMA since 2000. The rooftop has a
vegetable garden (closed Saturdays)
with heirloom vegetables and unusual
herbs, like salad burnet.
22–25 Jackson Ave., Long Island City,
NY 11101. Subway: G to 45 Rd.–
Court House Sq.

⓫ ROCKAWAY BEACH
One of the largest beaches on the East
Coast, a meeting spot for surfers from
around the world.
Rockaway Park, NY 11694.
Subway: A to Beach 67 St.

⓬ EAGLE STREET ROOFTOP FARM
A farm–yes, a farm!–on the roof of a
former Greenpoint factory, with fruit,
vegetables, chickens, rabbits, flowers,
and beehives.
44 Eagle St., Brooklyn, NY 11222.
Subway: G to Greenpoint Av.

⓭ WAVE HILL
A magnificent and immense (69 acres)
botanical garden, and a cultural center
overlooking the Hudson Palisades. The
Wave Hill café serves delicious dishes at
reasonable prices.
675 W 252nd St., Bronx, NY 10471.
MetroNorth to Riverdale

⓮ BRONX LITTLE ITALY ♥
The original neighborhood of New York's
Italian immigrants, more authentic than
Little Italy in Manhattan.
2396 Arthur Ave., Bronx NY 10458.
Subway: B, D to 182-183 Sts

⓯ EDGAR ALLAN POE COTTAGE
Home and garden of the *The Raven*'s
author. Edgar Allan Poe and his wife
moved into this pretty cottage, hoping
that the surrounding fresh air might help
cure her tuberculosis. Unfortunately,
she died in 1847, two years before the
mysterious death of her husband.
Grand Concourse and E 192nd St.,
Bronx, NY 10462.
Subway: B, D to Kingsbridge Rd.

P.S.1

QUENTIN VIJOUX

51 IT'S YOUR MAP !

You've covered fifty themes—playful, cultural, gastronomic, outdoorsy, inspired, classic, and secretive... The authors have shared their secrets and their personal favorites. Illustrators from around the world have each looked at the city from a personal angle: funny, offbeat, original, in love. It's your turn to adopt a theme, to "illustrate" the illustration, to fill in the blank page with memories, addresses, personal favorites, and perhaps the autographs of the beautiful people who you've met, thanks to the pages of this guide!

1

HOT DOGS

HOT DOGS

SANDRINE BONINI

NEW YORK ESSENTIALS

BEFORE YOU GO...
If you're travelling from overseas, remember to have a valid electronic biometric passport and to be in possession of an ESTA authorization or a visa.
Bring a power adapter.
Electricity: 110-115 V, 60 Hz.

NEW YORK CITY WEB
www.nycgo.com, www.nyc.gov

BOROUGHS
New York is divided into 5 districts (boroughs) : Manhattan, Bronx, Queens, Staten Island, and Brooklyn.

WHERE IS THE TOURIST OFFICE?
810 7th Ave., at the corner of 53rd St.
Open Monday to Friday, 8:30 a.m. to 6 p.m.; Saturday and Sunday from 9 a.m. to 5 p.m..
Telephone: (212) 484-1200.

WHAT ARE THE OPENING HOURS ?
Banks: Monday to Friday 9 a.m. to 5 p.m; sometimes Saturday from 9 a.m. to noon.
Bars: Usually open until 2 a.m., or 4 a.m. for after-hours bars and nightclubs.
Stores: Usually open daily from 10 a.m. to 7 p.m., sometimes closed Sundays or Mondays. Department stores: open daily from 9 a.m. to 8:30 p.m..
Museums: Usually open daily from 9 a.m. to 5 p.m..
Post Office: Monday to Friday 9 a.m. to 5 p.m.; some post offices are open on Saturday or even 24/7.
Restaurants: Usually open daily from 11 a.m. to 3 p.m., then from 5:30 p.m. to 11:30 p.m..
Public transport: 24/7.

WHAT'S THE RIGHT PRICE TO PAY?
Tipping: It is not included, and it is nearly obligatory, since the tip is often the greatest part of an employee's earnings. Around 15% of the bill; leaving less than 10% means that service was not up to par. If paying by debit card, indicate the amount of the tip on the line provided for the purpose. In bars, it's customary to leave $1 per drink; in hotels, $1 per bag for the porter, as well as a large tip for housekeeping. When the tip is included, it is indicated by the words "gratuity included."
Some examples of prices:
A cup of coffee: from $2 to $5.
A beer: $7.
A sandwich with drink: from $5 to $10.
A meal: from $20 to $40.
A bed in a youth hostel dorm: minimum, $35.
A standard room: from $150 to $200.
An average-distance taxi ride: $10.
A Broadway show: from $100 to $300.
Museum admission: from $8 to $20.
(Most museums offer a free or low-cost weekly hours).

Visitor's cards : CityPASS (**www.citypass.com**) and New York Pass (**www.newyorkpass.com**).
Taxes: prices mentioned always exclude tax. Add 8.375 % for services and consumer goods, 4.375 % for clothing under $110, 14.75 % for hotels.

It is not recommended to bring cash into the United States since the exchange is unfavorable onsite. International debit cards are sometimes necessary to pay for a hotel or rent a car.

HOW DOES PUBLIC TRANSPORTATION WORK?
Cost: A single ride: $2.75. A MetroCard is refillable as you go or there are special prices for unlimited travel: $31 for 7 days, $116.50 for 30 days. Each newly purchased MetroCard costs an additional $1. There is no charge to refill a MetroCard.
MetroCards can be used for subways and buses.
Bus: Operates 24/7. Frequency: approximately every 3 minutes during peak hours. Convenient for east-west links. Have the exact amount or a MetroCard; drivers do not give change. Press the stop button to get off.
The letter preceding the number of a bus indicates the area it serves (*M* for "Manhattan," *B* for "Brooklyn," etc.).
Subway: Operates 24/7. Frequency: every 2 to 5 minutes during peak hours (7:30 a.m. to 9 a.m. and 5 p.m. to 6:30 p.m.) and up to every 20 minutes between midnight and 6:30 a.m. Some stations are closed at night. Fast during peak hours; practical for north-south connections. The lines bear a number or a letter. The correct platform depends on the direction (downtown, toward the south; uptown, toward the north) or the destination (Brooklyn, Queens, etc.).
Local trains stop at every station; express trains only serve the main stations.
Yellow taxis: Pick-up charge: $2.50, then $0.40 every 0.2 miles (about 4 blocks) and $0.40 for stopped or slow traffic. Increase of $1 from 4 p.m. to 8 p.m. Monday to Friday and $0.50 every day from 8 p.m. to 6 a.m.. Bridge and tunnel tolls are paid by the customer. Tip: 15 to 30% of the taxi fare.

WHAT IS THE CALENDAR FOR HOLIDAYS AND CULTURAL EVENTS?
Holidays: January 1 (New Year's Day), 3rd Monday of January (Martin Luther King Jr. Day), 3rd Monday of February (Presidents' Day), last Monday of May (Memorial Day), July 4th (Independence Day), 1st Monday of September (Labor Day), 2nd Monday of October (Columbus Day), November 11 (Veterans Day), 4th Thursday of November (Thanksgiving Day), December 25 (Christmas Day).

January: Martin Luther King Jr. Day, 3rd Monday of the month; parade.
Restaurant Week: during one week at the end of the month, more affordable meals in the best restaurants. **Winter Antiques Show:** at the end of the month. **Chinese New Year,** between late January and early February; carnival in Chinatown.
February: Empire State Building Run-Up: early in the month, race to the 86th floor of the skyscraper; 1,575 steps to climb. **Black History Month:** an entire month of events revolving around African-American history.
March: St. Patrick's Day: the 17th, celebrating the patron saint of Ireland; parade on 5th Ave. **Macy's Flower Show:** at the end of the month, art in flowers in the store windows of Macy's department store.
Armory Show: during one week at the end of the month, major contemporary art fair at Piers 92 and 94.
New Director/New Film: during March and April, film festival; screenings at MoMA (Museum of Modern Art) and Lincoln Center.
April: Easter Sunday: end of March or April; parade on 5th Ave.
Artexpo New York: for three days, between the end of March and end of April, contemporary art show at Pier 94.
Central Brooklyn Jazz Festival: during the entire month, jazz concerts.
April or May: TriBeCa Film Festival: international film festival.
May: Five Boro Bike Tour: 1st Sunday of the month, cycling 67 km through five boroughs.
Memorial Day: last Monday of the month, in memory of the end of the Civil War.
June: Museum Mile Festival: 2nd Tuesday of the month, Upper East Side museums, free admission.
Puerto Rican Day Parade: 2nd Sunday of the month, on 5th Ave.
Lesbian and Gay Pride (NYC Pride): at the end of the month, concerts, film screenings and gigantic parade on 5th Ave.
Mermaid Parade: at the end of the month, on Coney Island, sea theme; homemade costumes, ball.
July: Independence Day: national holiday on the 4th; fireworks on Hudson and East Rivers.
Mostly Mozart Festival: from mid-July to end of August, free concerts at Lincoln Center.
Free Shakespeare in the Park: open-air theater in Central Park.
Lincoln Center Out of Doors: from mid-July to mid-August, free open-air concerts and ballets.
August: New York International Fringe Festival: two weeks of multidisciplinary performances (theater, music, dance, puppets, poetry, multimedia, etc.).
US Open: between the end of August and early September, one of four Grand Slam tennis tournaments, at Flushing Meadows.

Restaurant Week: during one week between end of August and early September. More affordable meals in the best restaurants.
September: Labor Day: 1st Monday of the month.
Feast of San Gennaro: for ten days in mid-month, in Little Italy, in memory of the first Italian immigrants.
October: Columbus Day: 2nd Monday of the month, celebrating the discovery of America by Christopher Columbus, parade on 5th Ave.
Halloween Parade: on the 31st, on 6th Ave.; impressive costumes and numerous festivities.
New York Film Festival: end of September to mid-October, at Lincoln Center.
BAM Next Wave Festival: mid-September to mid-December, theater, modern, and contemporary dance, classical music, at the Brooklyn Academy of Music.
November: TCS New York Marathon (some 50,000 participants): at the beginning of the month, across the five boroughs.
Thanksgiving Day: the 4th Thursday of the month, immense parade, giant helium balloons.
December: Holiday decorations, Christmas tree at Rockefeller Center. Gathering at Times Square on New Year's Eve, just before midnight, as the luminous ball descends, showing the date of the new year.

USEFUL NUMBERS

Emergencies: (fire, police, ambulance): 911.
Information: Dial 0 and ask the operator for the number, or dial 411.
Telephone: 3-digit area code + 7-digit telephone number. **Manhattan area codes:** 212, 646, and 917; **area code for other boroughs:** 718. **Local call** (when same area code): only the 7-digit telephone number when calling from a land line, all 10 digits if calling from a cell phone. **When calling another area code:** 1 + area code + telephone number. Numbers preceded by 800 or 1-800 are toll-free, and it is possible to call them from abroad by replacing them with the numbers 880 or 881, respectively.
To call New York from abroad: 1 + borough area code + 7-digit number. Dual-band cell phones do not work in the United States; only tri-band or quad-band phones will work.
Double charging for phone calls: the user pays part of an incoming or outgoing call.
Calls from pay phones: have the correct change.
To call collect: dial 0, ask the operator for a collect call, and give the number you wish to reach.
Prepaid phone cards: on sale in grocery stores, post offices, and at newsstands.

ILLUSTRATOR BIOGRAPHIES

50 MAPS is a crazy endeavor: to launch a collection of guides and to work with scores of illustrators, selected with love and constant passion. Some are well-known, others not, but all have been chosen for their creativity and originality. Here is a brief presentation of the paths each has followed.

MARION ALFANO

A graduate of the École Supérieure des Beaux-Arts of Bordeaux, Marion Alfano is a graphic designer and layout artist. She's interested in working on maps of cities and other places, real or imaginary.

MARIE ASSÉNAT

Marie Assénat, a French illustrator, lives in Brooklyn. She studied graphic arts and illustration in Brussels, where she graduated from La Cambre, École Nationale Supérieure des Arts Visuels. She draws and paints with gouache and India ink, inspired by themes such as animals, nature, daily life, and childhood.
She works for *AD Magazine*, *Clés*, *Elle*, *Psychologies Magazine*, *Télérama-Sortir à Paris*, the *New York Times*, the *New Yorker*, Bayard, Gallimard, L'École des loisirs, and Pastel.

XAVIER BARRADE

Xavier Barrade—graphic designer, illustrator and visual artist—studied at the École des Beaux-Arts in Paris. His projects are as varied as they are innovative. He works with volume, mixing different supports and techniques, and uses photography, paper, and his drawing talent to create works taking diverse forms from posters to video clips, including making models and 3D objects.
He works for the magazines *Amusement*, *Deleted Scenes*, *The Wire*, along with Canal + and the Orchestre de Paris.

SANDRINE BONINI

Sandrine Bonini graduated from the École Nationale Supérieure des Arts Décoratifs of Paris. She first worked in film animation, and then moved into illustration. She publishes books as either author or illustrator and also teaches illustration classes. She publishes with Éditions Autrement, Le Baron perché, L'École des loisirs, Picquier Jeunesse, Sarbacane, and Tana.

LISE BONNEAU

Lise Bonneau has been a freelance graphic designer since 2013. Born in Amiens, she studied visual arts at the ESAD after earning a degree in applied arts. She then left for Brussels to earn a masters in typography at La Cambre. Today, Lise splits her time between teaching, silkscreen, and wind instruments. She has been passionate about making models and paper since childhood. Her first artist's book, *Typop-up*, was published in June 2015.

BENOÎT CESARI

Benoît Cesari lives and works in Montpellier. He uses a felt-tip pen and black ink, then colors his drawing on the computer. He sometimes uses colored ink or watercolors. His illustrations mix humor and poetry. He works for *Anorak Magazine*, *Fricote Magazine*, *Mes premiers J'aime lire*, Éditions Frimousse, and the website gouvernement.fr.

MARINA DELRANC

After studying graphic design at the Arts Décoratifs of Paris, Marina Delranc became an art director. For the past ten years she has worked in publishing illustrated books. She is the art director for the *50 Maps* collection.

OLIVIER FONTVIEILLE

Olivier Fontvieille, a French graphic designer and illustrator, graduated from the École Estienne and the École Nationale Supérieure des Arts Décoratifs. He teaches typography and publishing design at the École de Communication Visuelle of Paris and works as an illustrator and graphic designer for publishing and the press. He works for the Édition Au diable vauvert, Belin, Fayard, Flammarion, Hachette, Labor et Fides, Éditions de La Martinière, and Mille et Une Nuits.

MAXIME GARCIA

Maxime Garcia is an illustrator, animated film director, and creator of comic books, posters, animated sequences, and concert-drawings. He studied engraving at Estienne, then illustration at the Arts Décoratifs of Strasbourg. He uses tools and mediums as diverse as pencil, engraving, or photography and enjoys staging laughable or grating situations. He works for France 3 Alsace and the French SNCF train company.

GREYGOUAR

Grégoire Gicquel, a French graphic designer and illustrator, is fascinated by the image and graphic design processes. He works regularly for the French press and uses various mediums such as posters, skateboards, or fabric. Inspired by street art, his style is characterized by the use of a distinct line, attention to details, and to colors. He works for *Challenges*, *Science & Vie Junior*, *Stratégies*, *The Good Life*, *The Hollywood Reporter*, *Time Out New York*, *Variety*, *XXI*, Colette, Tara Jarmon, and Timberland.

ÉLISE GODMUSE
Trained as a graphic designer, Élise lives in the Paris area. Today, as a freelancer, she illustrates book covers and works as a layout artist. Passionate about photography, especially portraits, she integrates photos into her graphic creations and illustrations.

PHILIPPE HALABURDA
Philippe Halaburda, a French painter, studied graphic design and visual arts in Paris. He creates abstract paintings using acrylic on various supports. He uses line, color, and the juxtaposition of shapes to create ensembles that burst with emotion.

BERNIE HOU
Bernie Hou is an American illustrator and comics author. With the use of photos and staging, he creates short series, such as the webcomic *Alien Loves Predator*, which has made him well known. He also draws cinema characters.

SARAH A. KING
Born in London, Sarah A. King studied graphic design at the University of Brighton. An illustrator and animated film director, she also does wood engravings and finds her sources of inspiration in nature and traveling. Letters and words play a major role in the composition of her drawings. She works for *Diplomat Magazine, LandScape Magazine, Oprah* magazine, *SC Magazine,* the *Guardian,* the *New York Times, The Untitled Magazine, Volume Magazine,* Taschen, BBC History, the San Francisco Museum of Modern Art, and the Big Chill Festival.

SOPHIE LEDESMA
Sophie Ledesma graduated from the École Supérieure d'Arts Graphiques of Paris. She is a textile designer and illustrator. Her bright and colorful drawings are compositions of solid shapes full of joyful, charming scenes. She works for *Cosmopolitan,* Éditions Fleurus, France Loisirs, Éditions de La Martinière, Éditions du Seuil, Nathan, and for the companies Du pareil au même, Ikea, and SFR.

AURÉLIE LEQUEUX
Graphic designer, visual arts teacher, and illustrator, Aurélie Lequeux lives and works in Paris. She thinks of illustration as a kind of grammar. For her, the juxtaposition of materials, colors, and shapes is a language, a plastic syntax.

PHILIPPE MARCHAND
The son of a publisher, Philippe Marchand was surrounded by images and books as a child. He studied graphic arts and book publishing in Italy, then international publishing in Great Britain. He was a freelance art director for 15 years until 2003, when he created his own studio, Olo. In 2007, he then cofounded Olo Éditions with Nicolas Marçais to give free rein to his love for different sorts of books.

MH
A graduate from Beaux-Arts, press illustrator and graphic artist MH creates little characters from clay that are full of humor. He places them in all sorts of situations, and he brings them to life by the use of modeling, drawing, and photography techniques. He works for, among others, *L'Expansion, Le Particulier,* MGEN, Nokia.

MIGUEL MONTANER
Miguel Montaner was born in Barcelona, where he studied graphic design and illustration. His style is synthetic and direct. He uses wide geometrical lines, soft and solid shapes, and lively colors that allow him to forcefully present his ideas. He places great importance on conceptual values and in the transmission of them, and perceives illustration as a means of communication. He notably works for *Adweek, Architects' Journal,* the *Boston Globe, Lexpert Magazine,* the *New York Times.*

MIGUEL PORLAN
Miguel Porlan was born in Barcelona, he mainly works for the international press. His illustrations are simple, marked by poetry and conveying strong ideas. He is an illustrator by vocation, but he has always thought of himself as a draftsman. His influences mainly come from comic books and graphic arts from the second half of the twentieth century. He is also passionate about music, which faithfully accompanies him during a good part of the creative process. His work has been published in the *New Yorker,* the *New York Times,* the *Wall Street Journal, Le Monde diplomatique Brasil, XXI,* and *France Culture Papiers.*

TANIA WILLIS
Tania Willis is an illustrator. She studied at the Royal College of Art, in London, then moved to Hong Kong. Passionate about map-making, she draws and paints travel illustrations. She has notably illustrated the walls of a Hong Kong hospital and a Dragonair airplane to celebrate the company's twentieth anniversary. Her maps and paintings, gay and luminous, in pastel tones, invite discovery and escape. She works for *Elle,* the *Guardian, Post Magazine, South China Morning Post,* the *Sunday Telegraph,* the *Observer Magazine, Time Magazine,* BBC Publications, Cartier, Channel V, Euro RSCG Ball Partnership, Li & Fung, and M&C Saatchi Hong Kong.

AGENCE LEZILUS

Since 2005, the Agence Lezilus has been presenting a selection of portfolios of a new generation of illustrators and graphic artists. Coming from street culture, animation, pixel art, contemporary design, etc., they bring a new way of looking at the world of communication.

JON BURGERMAN

Born in the United Kingdom, Jon Burgerman studied fine arts at the University of Nottingham, then moved to New York. This multitalented artist is both a designer and an illustrator. He has developed a somewhat abstract style using pop colors and presenting distorted characters outlined in black. His works are collected the world over; some are part of the permanent collections of the Victoria and Albert Museum and the Science Museum of London. He works for *Be Street, Paper* magazine, AOL, Mercedes-Benz, MTV, Nike, Pepsi, Pull-in, Puma, Rip Curl, Sony, and Sergeant Paper.

NIARK1

The Parisian illustrator Niark1, whose real name is Sébastien Féraut, is one of those artists who explores multiple fields. At ease both behind a screen or with a pencil in hand, over the years he has been able to develop his own universe, surrealistic and peopled with multicolored creatures straight out of his teeming imagination, while refining his ever-changing style. His work can be seen on music festival posters, clothing, skateboards, magazines, international publications, and in art galleries. He works for *Focus Mag, Graffiti Art, Göoo Mag, La TTongue Magazine*, the Éditions Cheval noir, Converse, the Foire de Lyon, L'Attrape-rêve, the Teatro alla Scala de Milan, Pictoplasma, Pull-in, Sergeant Paper, Syzygy, and Vibrations urbaines.

AGENCE ILLUSTRISSIMO

Illustrissimo, created in 1992 by Michel Lagarde, represents European illustrators, graphic designers, and animation artists from all backgrounds.

ICINORI

Mayumi Otero—whose mother is Japanese and father is Spanish—along with the French Raphaël Urwiller, graduated from the École Supérieure Arts Décoratifs of Strasbourg. They founded the experimental publisher Icinori, within which they develop their world and create unusual books, together or alone. Passionate about prints and silkscreening, nourished by the popular imagination and contemporary designs, they work with the same pleasure for the press, in publishing, or any other type of media. They collaborate with *Forbes, Le Tigre, L'Express*, the *New York Times, Wired, XXI*, Actes Sud, Helium, Nobrow, Sarbacane, and RMN.

GWENDAL LE BEC

Originally from Britanny, the illustrator Gwendal Le Bec studied graphic art at the École Duperré. In 2011, he was awarded the Pépite du meilleur album at the Salon de Montreuil for his book *Le Roi des oiseaux*. His drawings, colored or in black and white, are characterized by a sharp precise line, the play of light and of colors. He works for *Feuilleton, Le Monde*, the *New York Times*, the *Guardian*, Albin Michel, Gallimard, Walker Books, and Amnesty International.

JACOPO ROSATI

After studying at the Venice Art School, Jacopo Rosati gained experience as a multidisciplinary graphic artist at Studio Camuffo. His graphic universe then took shape and, with his limited palette and his not-as-immediately-identifiable world of cut felt, the Italian illustrator has a string of orders and enriches his creations every day. He works for *Berlin Poche, Das Magazin, Harvard Business Review, L'Express, New Internationalist, Parents Magazine, Playboy, Siemens Magazine, The Daily Telegraph, The Washington Post, TNT* magazine, *L'Espresso*, and *Vanity Fair*.

CHRISTIAN ROUX

Better known in the 1980s and 1990s under the pseudonym of "Cathy Millet," the French illustrator Christian Roux is back at the front of the graphic arts scene. This self-taught artist, who draws with India ink, is rich with a winding and atypical career. He has 30 years of graphic design experience behind him and a constantly evolving style, where the elegance of his lines and the freedom of his spirit make good partners. He works for *Alternatives internationales, La Vie, Le Monde, The Garden, Private Equity, XXI*, Albin Michel, and the Éditions du Seuil.

QUENTIN VIJOUX

A graduate of Duperré and Estienne schools, the Parisian illustrator Quentin Vijoux works for several communication agencies and draws for the international press. His "distinct lines" sometimes are married with compositions in volume or paper cut-outs. His first comic book, titled *Eugène*, was published by Éditions Michel Lagarde in 2013. He works for the *New York Times, Le Monde, XXI, Télérama, L'Obs, Psychologies Magazine, Doolittle, Terra Eco*, Bayard, Nathan, Google, Ogilvy, and Publicis.

JIM HANSON AGENCY

The Jim Hanson Agency, based in Chicago, has been working for 20 years with talented photographers and illustrators, passionate about art and creation.

MARI ARAKI

The Japanese illustrator Mari Araki considers herself to be both an artist and a storyteller. She graduated from the Art Center College of Design of Pasadena. She draws, paints, works in volume and plays with letters and images. She invites her characters to become the protagonists of her imaginary world with her colorful drawings, full of elegance and finesse. She has illustrated a book for Houghton Mifflin Harcourt publishers.

THOMAS BURNS

Thomas Burns is an American illustrator who graduated from the University of Florida in graphic design and in illustration from the College of Art and Design of Atlanta. He draws colorful scenes, whimsical and cheerful, teeming with thought-provoking details and ideas. He works for *Atlanta Magazine*, Coca-Cola, Georgia Conservancy, Insight Digital Media, MeadWestvaco, Monster Beverage, Netherworld, Peachtree City, Playboy Cable, PlayTell, the Tour de Georgia, and the Tour de Missouri.

HYESU LEE

Hyesu Lee is a joyful illustrator, awkward and "disorderly," who lives in New York. Thanks to her work, she loves to share the beauty and happiness hidden in the world. She has published four books and created illustrations for various magazines and advertising agencies, including the *Boston Globe*, the *New Yorker*, *Time Out New York*, Chobani, Apple, Blue Moon, the *Washington Post* and Nissan Japan.

GARANCE AGENCY

Garance is an illustration agency based in the United States, representing a group of international artists among the most renowned in illustration. In advertising, press, and publishing, the artists lend their talents to a long list of multinational companies (Swatch, Coca-Cola, Christian Dior, etc.).

BENEDITA FEIJÓ

Benedita Feijó is one of the most popular Portuguese graphic designers. After studying at London's prestigious Central Saint Martins College of Art and Design, she worked as an illustrator for advertising and major brands. She has also created a line of colorful objects. She works with dreamlike collages, inspired by the richness of nature and of the city.

ÉRIC GIRIAT

Éric Giriat, a graduate of ESAG, calls himself a designer without geographical, aesthetic, or thematic borders; a creator of often playful and poetic images, where painting, collages, photos, and pixels can mix, but where the style remains very recognizable. He works in all sorts of fields, from fashion to economy by way of politics, psychology, children's publishing, decoration, and even portraiture. He also collaborates with young fashion designers and major labels such as Joop. He works with *Elle*, *Better Homes & Gardens*, *Journal Für die Frau*, *Les Échos*, *Le Monde*, *Le Nouvel Économiste*, *Nova*, *Petra*, *Première*, *Psychologies Magazine*, *The Economist*, Albin Michel, Belfond, Nathan, J'ai lu, Pocket, Robert Laffont, and Celltech.

LORENZO PETRANTONI

The unique illustrations of Lorenzo Petrantoni mix his passion for graphic design and his fascination for the nineteenth century. Born in 1970 in Genoa, Lorenzo studied graphic arts in Milan before starting his career as an art director in advertising agencies in France, then in Italy, where he produced campaigns for major brands. In 2009 he decided to devote all of his time to his work as an illustrator. Lorenzo Petrantoni uses images, drawings, and typography taken from old books and dictionaries that he unearths at bookstores and flea markets. His work, regularly praised by the press, mixes eras, playing with them to give new life to forgotten words, events, and people, or to reappropriate the news. His clients include the *New York Times*, the *New Yorker*, *Businessweek*, the *New Scientist*, *Wired*, *BBC*, the *Guardian*, *Time Out New York*, *Il Sole 24 Ore*, *Internazionale Magazine*, Coca-Cola, Nike, Burton, and Nespresso.

ACKNOWLEDGEMENTS

Copyright Éditions would like to thank all of the illustrators who participated in this project, as well as their agents (Marie Joanne Wimmer, Evgueni Kalatchev, Nicolas Pitzalis) for their help, their enthusiasm, and their professionalism.

PHOTOGRAPHIC CREDITS
Shutterstock © alien-tz: pp. 1, 2, 106, 107, 108, 110, 112; © balabolka: p. 109; © Blu67design: p. 111.
Independent illustrators: © Benoît Cesari: front cover, p. 5; © Philippe Marchand: pp. 7, 37; © Olivier Fontvieille: pp. 9, 59, 71 (necklace © Vladimirfloyd/Fotolia and portrait: © Ramzi Hachicho/Fotolia); © Philippe Halaburda: p. 11; © Greygouar: pp. 15, 65; © Élise Godmuse: pp. 17 (machine: © Fotolia/lgarts), 47; © Aurélie Lequeux: p. 19; © Marina Delranc: pp. 41, 57 (map background: © Shutterstock/Roberto A Sanchez); © Miguel Porlan: pp. 27, 91; © Xavier Barrade: p. 31; © Sophie Ledesma: pp. 21, 95; © Marie Assénat: pp. 35, 77; © Tania Willis: p. 39; © MH: p. 43; © Maxime Garcia: pp. 49, 63, 97; © Bernie Hou: p. 51; © Marion Alfano: pp. 69, 99; © Miguel Montaner: p. 73; © Sarah A. King: pp. 75, 93; © Lise Bonneau: p. 83; © Sandrine Bonini: p. 105 and cover pages.
Jim Hanson Agency © Hyesu Lee: pp. 55, 87; © Mari Araki: p. 61 (photo, © Shutterstock/glamour); © Thomas Burns: p. 101.
Agence Illustrissimo © Gwendal Le Bec: pp. 23, 25; © Christian Roux: pp. 29, 53; © Icinori: p. 67; © Quentin Vijoux: pp. 85, 103; © Jacopo Rosati: p. 89.
Agence Lezilus © Niark1: p. 33; © Jon Burgerman: p. 45.
Garance Agency © Éric Giriat: p. 79; © Benedita Feijó: p. 81; © Lorenzo Petrantoni: p. 13.

Original concept and direction of the collection: Philippe Marchand.
Artistic direction and graphic design: Marina Delranc.
Editorial director: Laura Stioui, assisted by Guénola Sacher.
Publishers: Audrey Busson and Capucine Viollet.
Layout artist: Marion Alfano, assisted by Aurélie Lequeux.
Copyediting and proofreading: Emmanuelle Desnoyer and Sabine Terliska.
Photoengraving: Peggy Huynh-Quan-Suu.
Production: Stéphanie Parlange.

First published in the United States of America in 2016 by
Universe Publishing, a division of Rizzoli International Publications, Inc.
300 Park Avenue South, New York, NY 10010
www.rizzoliusa.com

Originally published in French as *New York en 50 cartes* in 2015 by En Voyage Editions

Original idea and creation © 2015 Copyright Éditions

2016 2017 2018 2019 / 10 9 8 7 6 5 4 3 2 1

ISBN: 978-0-7893-3117-5

Library of Congress Catalog Control Number: 2015955244

Printed in Malaysia